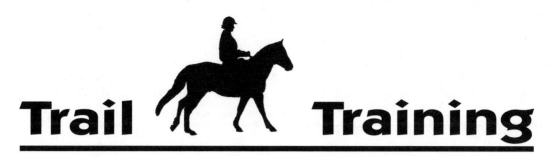

Trail Training

for the Horse and Rider

Judi Daly

Photo © K. S. Swigart

Alpine Publications

Trail Training for the Horse and Rider
Copyright © 2004 by Judi Daly

Library of Congress Cataloging-in-Publication Data

Daly, Judi, 1965-
   Trail training for horse and rider / Judi Daly.
       p. cm.
     ISBN 1-57779-057-X
   1. Trail riding. 2. Horses--Training. I. Title.

   SF309.28.D36 2004
   798.2'3--dc22   2004046358

The information contained in this book is complete and accurate to the best of our knowledge. All recommendations are made without guarantee on the part of the author or Alpine Publications, Inc. The author and publisher disclaim any liability with the use of this information.

For the sake of simplicity, the terms "he" or "she" are sometimes used to identify an animal or person. These are used in the generic sense only. No discrimination of any kind is intended toward either sex.

Many manufacturers secure trademark rights for their products. When Alpine Publications is aware of a trademark claim, we identify the product name by using initial capital letters.

This book is available at special quantity discounts for breeders and for club promotions, premiums, or educational use. Write for details.

Design: Laura Newport
Cover Photo: © K. S. Swigart
Editing: Deborah Helmers
Photographs: by the author unless otherwise credited
Illustrations: Holly Zelwalk

First printing May 2004

1 2 3 4 5 6 7 8 9 0

Printed in the United States of America.

Contents

To my sister, Ellen Daly

Preface

Why did I write this book? As a young girl, I dreamt of horses day and night. It was almost always the same dream. I would be riding out on a wooded trail on a lovely day in May, with the sun shining, the birds singing, wild flowers everywhere . . .

My first horse was an old Morgan named Brandy, given to me by my aunt. I found a place to keep him near some great trails, and it looked like my dream would come true. On our first trip out, I found I was the proud owner of a barn sour, hardheaded, confirmed runaway horse that was probably given to me because no one else wanted him. My third attempt at riding him on trail climaxed when he turned on a dime, ran into the street, and followed the yellow centerline at a gallop for a quarter mile down the road before I got him under control.

I went back to the drawing board. We spent many weeks working together in the arena to improve my skills and teach him to listen better. I talked to many people and read whatever I could find. I was surprised that I found very little to read that was of much use to me. Finally, I psyched myself into keeping my dream alive. My hard work paid off, and I was rewarded with two years of great trail riding before his death at the age of 24.

While I was out on trail, I encountered many things, got into a number of difficult situations and didn't know what to do. I managed to muddle through them and come out all right, but maybe I was just lucky.

So, why did I write this book? So I can help other people to achieve their dream or explore a different area of horsemanship that they may be unprepared for. Over the years, I have found many people who want to trail ride but are afraid. Some of them tried it a few times and had such bad experiences that they just gave up. A few just concentrated on a different kind of riding, but a lot of them actually gave up on horses altogether. Their horse would stand in his stall, neglected, for a year or two before they decided to sell him. My advice may help to give people like this the confidence to attain their dream. I hope to encourage them to form a training program suited to their situation to solve their problems and to prevent them from muddling through it like I had to.

Just having an idea of what to do in a bad situation can keep a rider from panicking and may possibly prevent an accident from happening. If just one accident in the whole horse kingdom is prevented because of this book, all the hours of work I put into it will be worth it.

Much of this book is about training because I don't believe in just hopping on a horse and "cowboying" down the trail. I feel a good trail horse is made, not born. Of course, I've seen a lot of lucky people buy a horse and never have a problem trail riding. In most cases, those people benefited by someone else's hard work or were just plain lucky. Horseback riding is too dangerous to rely on luck.

Safety is behind everything I recommend. Trail riding is riskier than any other form of riding because we go so far from home and a minor accident can escalate into something serious if there is no help readily available.

So read the book, consider my advice, adapt it for your horse and your environment and open the door to miles and miles of trails waiting to be explored. It's really worth it.

Judi Daly

Acknowledgments

Thanks to all the people who shared their many experiences with me. I have learned so much just by listening to them. There are far too many to list, but I must give special thanks to Sharon Boros who shared so many of her adventures with her Arabian mares.

Of course, I couldn't have written this book without the wonderful horses that have touched my life. Our horses are truly our best teachers. In particular, I want to thank Cruiser, the scared horse; Brandy, the out-of-control horse; Mingo, the stubborn horse; and Ranger, the mysterious horse.

After going on a trail ride on one of my horses, Susan Kandzer offered to read the manuscript when it was in its formative stage. It opened her eyes to all the potential dangers of trail riding, yet she came out and rode with me many times after that. Her enthusiasm for this book aided in pushing it out of its infant stage and into maturity.

I must also thank the many friends who encouraged me along the way. My sister, Ellen Daly, believed in me more than I believed in myself. She listened to all my ideas years before they were put on paper, and was my guinea pig, testing my theories on her own horse, Ranger.

Additionally, I want to thank the people who allowed me to take photos of them and their horses, and Holly Zelwalk for providing the lovely illustration.

I am deeply appreciative of Cleveland MetroParks for allowing horses on the trails. Not only did I learn a wealth of information riding those trails, they helped me fulfill a life-long dream of owning a trail horse even though I live in the city. The bulk of the photos in this book were taken in these lovely parks.

Section I

Riding on the Trail

CHAPTER ONE

Why Trail Ride?

Trail riding is the fastest growing pastime for equestrians, in part because the options for this kind of riding are so varied. Loose your imagination for a moment: Picture yourself and your horse riding quietly on your regular trail, greeting other frequent users, starting or ending your day with the joy of familiar sights, scents and sounds, watching those small changes that herald the shifting of the seasons. Now envision a long day of spectacular mountain riding with new friends, ending with laughter and companionship around a campfire under the stars. And now imagine yourself far from civilization, rounding yet another twist in a deep canyon in the Southwest's redrock country, while hundreds of feet above you soars a glorious arch. Or maybe you would prefer the excitement and hard work of driving cattle on a working ranch. Or you want to ride on a beach, waves crashing nearby...see Patagonia via horseback...tour wine country in France.... Once you start exploring the world of trail riding, the sky is literally the limit.

THE VARIED BENEFITS OF TRAIL RIDING

Why trail ride? Simply put, it's fun! Riding the trails is a great way to escape the hustle and bustle of the fast-paced society we live in, in a way that competing in horse shows doesn't even approach. There is no better way to get to know your horse, get good exercise and commune with nature than to trail ride. It is relaxing, stress relieving, and good for the soul. So much of our lives zooms by at 110 miles per hour—a leisurely ride on the trail is about as far away from the hectic pace of society as we can get. With beautiful scenery and the perfect companion (our horse), this can be a quiet, healing time that helps prepare us to face the world again in a much better frame of mind.

There was a time when owning a horse was a symbol of freedom. It was a way we could travel great distances, visit friends and see the world, much in the same way the car allows today. The horse is still a symbol of freedom, but now it is the freedom to get away from the world

Riders ascend Slick Rock on the Outlaw Trail. Photo © K. S. Swigart.

An evening ride with the family dog alongside is a great stress reducer. Photo © Kim Andrews.

as we know it. The horse is truly the symbol of escape, and the trails are the greatest places to go when escaping.

The benefits of trail riding do not stop with pure pleasure. Anyone can integrate it into their training plans re-gardless of which aspect of horseman-ship they currently pursue. John Lyons, world-renowned horse trainer, advo-cates doing the bulk of training, both beginning and advanced, out on the trail.

In part this is because trail riding is great for the horse's mental health. Bore-dom in the training routine can con-tribute to resistance and lack of impul-sion, and impulsion is vital in all forms of competitive riding. Trail riding wakes most horses up and gives them an inter-est in the work, resulting in natural im-pulsion with very little effort from the rider. Just taking one day a week from your training routine to trail ride can make a world of difference with your horse. I've had wonderful results by working in the ring for half an hour, and when my horse does well, I reward him immediately by taking him out of the arena for a short trail ride. I know a woman who trains the opposite way. She starts with a short trail ride to warm her horse up and then returns to the arena to school her horse.

Several competitive upper level dressage riders insist trail riding is not just helpful, but essential to their training. One woman who competes her Arabian in the third level told me she wasn't able to achieve good extension in the dressage ring until she tried to get it on the trail. Her horse is a joy to watch whether in the ring or out in the park. He has a marvelous attitude that trail riding only encourages.

A routine that is too strict, in addition to leading to boredom, can cause a horse to be nervous in new situations. On the trail a horse is exposed to many new sights and sounds, giving him a more open mind. He will be more likely to take diversity in stride and will generally be more relaxed, including when in the show ring.

Trail riding also builds stamina in both the horse and the rider. Most riders and horses become bored if working in an arena for more than an hour, yet it is easy to ride out on a trail for two to three hours. Riding for longer lengths of time conditions a horse far better than short workouts. I've seen show horses that seem to give their all simply to last in a twenty-minute class. On the other hand, I know trail horses that are ridden to shows, compete all day and are ridden back home without any sign of weariness.

Of course, you don't stop training when you are trail riding, because anything you do with your horse at any time is training. Trail riding gives you a chance to educate your horse naturally. A smart rider takes advantage of the terrain to accomplish other goals in training. There is nothing like riding up and down hills to encourage balance and teach a horse to step with his hind legs well underneath. One woman "works the hills" several days before a dressage competition for this very reason.

Traveling on uneven ground teaches a horse balance as well as giving him an awareness of his surroundings. He

Trail riders can use open areas to practice circles and bending.

Trail riding definitely encourages impulsion. Photo © John Burkett.

learns to be careful where he steps. The more you trail ride, the less your horse will stumble. A horse that has been worked exclusively in an arena can become careless under all but ideal conditions.

More specific goals can be worked on, too. Collection can be worked on going away from home. Conversely, coming home is a great time to work on extension, since most horses are more enthusiastic when going back to the barn. I've had wonderful results from working on transitions on the trail. A mile of transitions on an interesting path isn't at all boring for your horse compared to the equivalent in an arena. Lateral bending can be practiced on corners, around trees and bushes, and in open fields. Picking up a correct lead is very natural on a sharp bend on the trail. I find it much easier to teach the correct lead on the trail rather than in a corner of an arena. By training with specific goals in mind instead of plodding aimlessly along, you will encourage obedience, free forward movement and impulsion. You will also help your horse gain confidence, a quality valuable anywhere he might go.

THE DRAWBACKS OF TRAIL RIDING

There are few valid reasons not to trail ride your horse. The biggest reason, by far, is the increased risk for accidents, combined with the possible difficulty in getting help. Having some knowledge of first aid or riding close to civilization can minimize the risk. Also, if the horse is a valuable show animal, a scar could mar his career or an injury ruin a show season. The owner may not want to take the unnecessary risk. In fact, though, trail riders often go for years without ever having a serious problem. It's up to each owner to weigh the potential risks and make his or her own decision. One of the main goals of this book is to make riders aware of potential dangers and to give suggestions on how to deal with difficulties when they do occur as well as how to avoid them when possible.

Another deterrent to trail riding is a horse that misbehaves. However, few horses that can be ridden well in the safe confines of an arena are lost causes on the trail.

A horse that bucks, rears, balks and generally misbehaves at home probably will not behave any better on the trail. The problem should be solved in the arena first. At times, however, a horse may surprise you. One summer I worked with a three-year-old Arabian filly that was very uncooperative and hyper in the ring but was a dream out on the trail. From the beginning, she gave me few problems when out of the arena.

PROTECTING YOUR TRAILS

The most common obstacle to trail riding is the lack of available trails. Many people have to trailer their horses to get to good, safe trails. I pay a premium to board my horses next to a very large, extensive park system so I can have easy access to good trails. If you also are fortunate enough to have convenient access to trails, be sure not to take them for granted. Take care of the them better than if they were your own, because trails can quickly become closed to horses. If you do cause any damage, offer to fix or pay for it. Always leave things exactly the way you found them. Good trails are a treasure to be cherished.

Crossing the Platte River. Photo © K. S. Swigart.

Find out if there are any active groups that promote trail riding in your area and join them. If you can, participate in their activities. Chances are very good that you will make some great friends who enjoy trail riding as much as you do.

Even if you don't have the time to become actively involved with the group, your membership counts. These groups work to keep trails open to horses and also are involved in opening and maintaining new trails. Trail riders usually ride where they are not necessarily visible; after all, we want to get away from the world. Unfortunately, that means we aren't noticed as much as other user groups. By uniting, we form a voice that state and local governments will listen to. I am a member of the Ohio Horse Council. We keep track of our miles, and at the end of the year, we turn in our records to the state and the local park systems, so they will know how much we actually do ride out on their trails. This way, they are more responsive to our needs.

Once you start trail riding, an exciting world opens to you—a world of new and varied opportunities, sights, sounds, experiences and friends. Enjoy your adventures!

CHAPTER TWO

Preparing to Ride

WHAT KIND OF HORSE FOR TRAIL RIDING?

One of the real joys of trail riding is that any horse that is sound can make a great trail horse. I've seen everything out on the trail from the standard saddle-horse breeds to Percherons, Friesians and mules. Gaited horses are becoming very popular because of their comfortable way of going. The only prerequisite for a good trail horse is soundness and a good mind.

Size doesn't matter. Although small horses are frowned on in so many horse sports, on trails small and big horses do equally well. If you are thinking of purchasing a horse to trail ride, keep in mind that it's best to have one that you can mount easily from the ground. The ideal size of horse is the size that fits you the best.

Looks also aren't important. Some very ugly horses that would be laughed out of the show ring thrive on the trail and even in competitive trail rides. Unlike the show ring, a horse is not penalized for petty conformation faults that do not affect soundness. Oversized ears, coarse features and unsuitable tails don't mean a thing on the trail—soundness and good manners are far more valuable

than halter-class beauty. Conformation is important only to the extent it affects the ride.

The walk of a good trail horse is comfortable, without clipping, forging or overreaching, all of which can cause injuries. Proper conformation will also enable a horse to go farther with less discomfort to himself, while poor conformation may cause trouble. For example, a horse with a longer than normal back may suffer some back pain from a three-hour ride. A trail horse's withers should be well shaped to keep the saddle in position; no one wants to have to stop to constantly readjust the saddle when going downhill or worry about it slipping while mounting.

Lastly, the horse's feet must be sound. Some horses have very tough feet and may only need front shoes or possibly no shoes at all for the amount of riding done and the terrain covered. If shoes are necessary, it is vitally important that your horse have a good quality hoof that will hold the shoe in place. A horse with poor quality hooves will throw shoes far more often. This can be a big problem if you are far from home.

Horses of any gender can do well on the trail. Geldings tend to have very consistent behavior and are an excellent

Quarter Horse followed by a Missouri Foxtrotter. Photo © Kim Andrews.

Dottie is out for a ride on her Tennessee Walker, Pistol.

A trail horse should walk quietly with a loose rein.

choice for a new rider. When working with stallions or mares, however, there are some special considerations. Due to their unpredictability, stallions rarely should take part in group rides, although they can be terrific by themselves. If you must ride a stallion in a group, or if you are worried about meeting mares while riding alone on a stallion, be especially alert and attentive in the springtime—when mares go in season, the problem is much greater. To keep their horses from getting distracted, racehorse trainers will put Vick's VapoRub on the edges of their colts' nostrils to mask the smell of the mares.

Also be aware that a mare can behave quite differently from her norm when she comes into heat, which happens about every twenty-one days—a sweet, mild-mannered mare may become a kicking, irritable mount when around other horses. On those days, you may want to avoid large groups altogether, so that you and your mare both can have a more enjoyable ride. Whenever I work with a mare, I keep track of her heat cycles so I don't get taken by surprise.

The age of the horse is of little consideration, other than that it complement the experience of the rider. At least one of the rider-mount pair should be experienced; novice riders should not be paired with young or green horses. Older horses do quite well on the trail. Indeed, this type of riding can extend the useful life of the horse, since it keeps him active yet is less stressful than many other equestrian events.

PROPER ATTIRE

When considering attire for trail riding, anything goes as long as it is safe and comfortable. The most important items are what's on the top and what's on the bottom: that is, your helmet and your footwear.

I highly recommend wearing a helmet, even if you ride Western. One-fifth of all equestrian accidents involve the head, sixty-five percent of all hospitalized horse-related accidents are head injuries, and sixty percent of equestrian-related deaths are due to the same cause. Wearing a proper helmet can prevent most head injuries. There is no such thing as a horse that is safe enough or a rider who is experienced enough that a helmet isn't necessary. *Everyone* should wear a helmet every single time they ride, whether on the trail or at home. Unexpected things happen.

One day while riding in the indoor arena at a boarding stables, I saw a board sticking out from the wall. My horse

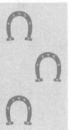

The use of helmets on the trail is becoming more and more common; at least half the people I see riding on the trail use them. By wearing one, you encourage other people to do the same.

Cruiser was not yet responsive to my leg aids. Try as I might to get him to move over, he still scraped up against the board. It hooked my stirrup leather and pulled me right off the back of the saddle. No matter that I was experienced or that I knew the "proper" way to fall to avoid serious injuries, I fell and hit my head. In this case, my helmet may have saved me a trip to the hospital. I drove home with a smile on my face.

It's true that not long ago the helmets available were of little use except for appearances. They were used in the show ring as part of the required costume. However, with the new SEI (Safety Equipment Institute) standard helmets, you can now be sure your helmet is actually doing some good. Many of the SEI helmets are extremely light-weight and have vents for cooling, making them quite comfortable to wear. Western riders who worry about looking silly with an English helmet have no excuse—there are now Western-style helmets available.

Your helmet should be level from the front to the back, with the front edge about an inch from the top of your eyebrows. It should fit snugly and not slide freely about the head, and it absolutely should not be removable once the strap is hooked up. It is important that you always keep the strap fastened. A helmet is useless if it falls off your head in an accident. An added benefit to wearing a helmet is that the visor will protect your face and eyes from the sun and will keep rain off your face.

The other required element of trail riding apparel is some sort of heeled footwear. The heel will help prevent your foot from getting caught in the stirrup. I usually ride English, and I like to wear tall boots. I don't get leather because I ride through too much water and mud; I am simply too lazy to take proper care of leather boots. The synthetic

boots don't require the same care and are much less expensive.

Aside from the requirement of a heel, the type of footwear chosen is just a matter of personal preference. Some English riders like the shorter paddock boots. I like the tall ones because they protect my legs from mosquitoes in the summer. There is also a myriad of nice Western boots to choose from. Some people prefer riding tennis shoes; these are usually well made and have that all-important heel.

The other clothes you wear need only be comfortable and suitable for the weather. Watch for any wrinkles on your leg wear that may rub against your skin and cause discomfort on long rides. Also be sure to layer your clothing so you are prepared for weather changes.

TACK

Your horse can wear any well-fitting tack as long as it is clean and in good repair. With no judges setting the standards, a whole world of tack is available to you in all kinds of different styles and colors. Just as many people can be seen trail riding in English equipment as in Western—once again, this is simply a matter of preference. I've also seen Australian, plantation, saddle seat and military saddles. (Recently, I've been using an old Japanese military saddle from WWII, which both my horse and I find very comfortable.) Many people swear by synthetic saddles and bridles because of their lightness and easy care, while others prefer traditional leather. As long as it is comfortable for you and fits the horse, your tack is a matter of personal preference. Keep in mind that particular terrain may call for extra items, such as breast collars for steep hills.

A first aid kit should be considered part of your required attire. This will contain the basics, such as antiseptics and bandaging materials, for both you and your horse. Many riders also wear a small survival pouch on their own bodies for those times when they have made an unplanned dismount and their horses are happily trotting away with the complete supplies. This smaller pack contains such items as cotton balls coated with antibiotic ointment, aspirin, adhesive tape, a space blanket, waterproof matches, flashlight, tablets to purify drinking water, and a nutritional bar.

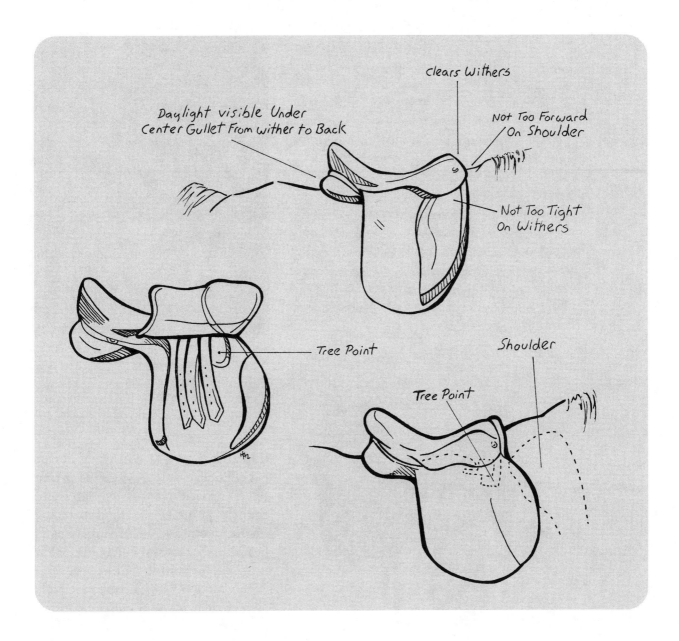

If your horse is not moving well or exhibits behavior problems, it may be the result of an ill-fitting saddle. Saddle your horse and check that the lowest part of the seat is in the center of the saddle where you sit and that it is level. A correctly fitted saddle will have even pressure on all of the parts that come in contact with your horse's back. Nowhere should it be touching the spine. Also, compare your saddle from side to side to make sure it is even and straight.

When girthed, make sure the back of your saddle does not ride up when you push down on the horn or pommel. This would indicate that the tree is too wide. A saddle that swings side to side also indicates a too-wide tree. A saddle that sits high over the withers is too narrow. On a new saddle, while mounted, check to see if there is two to three fingers' width between the pommel and your horse's withers. This will flatten with use. A used saddle should have two fingers' width between the pommel and withers.

After you ride, look for roughed up parts of hair or uneven sweat marks on

Poorly fitting saddles affect a horse and his performance long before sores become apparent. The goal is to have a saddle not only that fits the horse at rest by distributing its pressure evenly, but also that moves with him as he moves. Pain in a horse's back causes him to alter his carriage and way of going, and can result in lameness. His attitude may change and his performance deteriorate. Simply adding more or thicker saddle pads in an attempt to "even out" the pressure may actually worsen the problem, or else merely move it to another area of his back. If you have questions about the fit of your saddle, consult an expert.

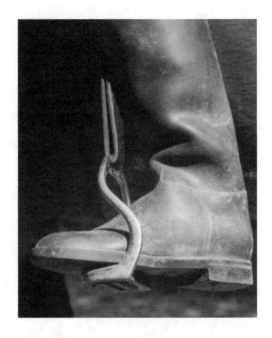

One type of English safety stirrup.

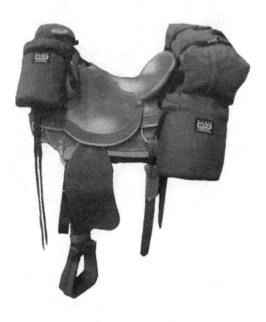

Trail saddle with saddlebags and pommel bags.

your horse. These, too, can be signs of an ill-fitting saddle. Over an extended period of time, your horse's hair will actually turn white wherever there is an excessive amount of pressure in one spot.

Saddle placement is also very important, especially with English saddles. A Western saddle, if correctly fitting, will usually slide back from the withers and find its proper place on your horse's back. English saddles are often placed too far forward. For proper placement, the tree point of the English saddle should be one and a half to two fingers behind your horse's shoulder blade. If it is too far forward, it will impede your horse's motion and if it is too far back, it will irritate his back muscles.

This is only a rough guide to help you. If you are unsure, and have any concerns about how your saddle fits, check with a professional saddle fitter.

English riders now have the option of equipping their saddles with stirrups that prevent the rider's foot from getting caught in case of a fall. It's something you should consider. A horse in an arena may not take off running if his rider falls off, and even if he does run, he can't go very far. Out on trail, though, many horses are very eager to hightail it all the way home. Getting dragged is much more likely. There are several different types of these stirrups, so check your

This saddle has a sheepskin seat pad and saddlebags attached. Photo © B. J. McKinney.

A fanny pack secured behind the seat was used on this horse that had never worn saddlebags. A water-bottle holder is also snapped to the saddle. Photo © B. J. McKinney.

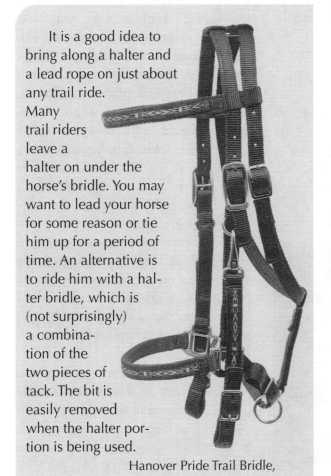

It is a good idea to bring along a halter and a lead rope on just about any trail ride. Many trail riders leave a halter on under the horse's bridle. You may want to lead your horse for some reason or tie him up for a period of time. An alternative is to ride him with a halter bridle, which is (not surprisingly) a combination of the two pieces of tack. The bit is easily removed when the halter portion is being used.

Hanover Pride Trail Bridle,
Courtesy of The Stage Coach West.

A pommel bag is on the front and a jacket tied to the back of this trail rider's saddle. Photo © B. J. McKinney.

local tack shop or catalog and see what is available.

You may opt to get a safety stirrup that has a rubber piece that pops out in an accident. Try to avoid riding whenever that part is missing from the stirrup or you may find yourself unexpectedly parting company with your horse. A friend once noticed while out on a trail ride that the rubber piece had popped off. Since she wasn't very far from home, Sharon decided to keep riding. She figured the missing piece wouldn't make a difference since she wasn't planning on going any faster than a walk. Wouldn't you know it? Her horse spooked, and her foot slipped out of the stirrup. She was still in the saddle, but before she could recover herself, her horse spooked a second time in the opposite direction. That's all it took, and Sharon flew out of the saddle.

PROPER GROOMING

Unlike in a show ring, your horse is only going to get dirty out on the trail, so there's no reason to groom him to perfection unless you want to. The only grooming necessary before a ride is to clean your horse's feet, inspect his whole

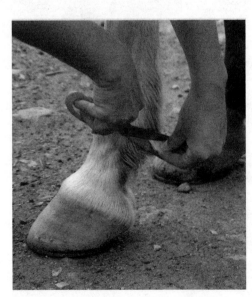

If you don't have a clippers, use a scissors to neaten your horse's fetlock.

body for any sores or swelling, and clean the saddle and girth area immaculately. Dirt or dried sweat under the saddle area can create problems. I can get my horse cleaned and tacked up in less than fifteen minutes. I don't like to rush, but often there is a limited amount of time to ride after work. I clean my horses up after a ride as well, so they often look better after the ride than before it. Also, the next time I go out to ride, I won't have as much work to get them ready.

On rainy days I work on mane and tail combing. I use untangling conditioners heavily to preserve my horses' long manes and tails. Conditioners also make it easier to remove any burrs that are caught. Although it is easier to care for short hair, I like manes and tails long for their protection against insects. You may want to consider letting your horse grow his mane and tail longer for this reason alone, even if it isn't proper for your breed. A trail rider doesn't need to worry about fashion or show regulations.

It is smart to keep your horse's fetlocks trimmed to help keep them free from mud and ice. Your horse's legs will also dry more quickly. Scissors work fine if your horse doesn't like clippers or if they are too expensive. I also use scissors to trim the bridle path.

The first thing I usually do when I get back from a ride is untack my horse and put him right in his stall. Some horses will not urinate with riders on their backs unless they are desperate. By giving the horse a few minutes alone, he can take care of any necessary business.

After his break, brush off any mud and dried sweat. At times your horse may be too wet to clean well. If it is warm enough, you may want to rinse him off. Soap isn't necessary. I usually don't have the luxury of giving my horse a full bath either because I am short of time or because in the dead of summer, baths are often banned at our barn due to a shortage of water. That is when I just take a bucket of water and a sponge to wipe off the sweaty areas. In the cooler weather, you can let the sweat dry thoroughly while you do barn chores, and then it will brush off with a currycomb very easily. Of course, you should clean your horse's feet after every ride.

That being said, don't think you can get away with hardly any grooming simply because your horse isn't a show horse. Try to schedule a deep grooming at least a couple times a week. Give your horse a really good currying to get out the buildup of dried sweat and dander. This is particularly important when your horse is shedding his winter or his summer coat. Brush him to get that beautiful, healthy shine on his coat. Not only will your horse enjoy it it will keep him looking his best. A deep grooming is perfect for the days you don't intend to ride. It gives you the opportunity to spend good, quality time with your horse.

The best way to keep your horse looking good is to feed him quality food, exercise him regularly and keep his worming up to date. A healthy horse that is seldom given a deep grooming will shine better than an ill-kept horse with hours of grooming.

After a long ride, your horse may feel just as achy as you do. He would appreciate a good massage. It is not hard to massage horses, and there are plenty of good books that will show you the basics. I particularly like the massages that Linda Tellington-Jones teaches in her books. They are easy to learn and very effective. Massaging gives you a chance to find any specific soreness your horse may have and give him some relief from it. By watching his expressions and actions closely, you will find out what hurts, what he likes and where he is ticklish. It's a great way to end your day together.

To measure the length of the bridle path, hold the ear back against the neck. Photo from Understanding Showmanship *by Laurie Tuskauskas © 2001.*

FOOT PROTECTION

Most trail horses will need some protection for their feet. If you prefer not to shoe your horse, pull-on "boots" can be purchased at tack stores or through mail order catalogs.

First, thoroughly clean the hoof. Then put on the boot and tighten it according to the instructions. One such boot, manufactured by EasyCare, Inc., is the Boa Horse Boot. This boot uses the same materials and technology as modern athletic shoes and provides excellent traction. The Boa Horse Boot is designed to be used on bare feet rather than over shoes, and is much easier to apply and remove than the Easyboot.

The Boa Horse Boot. Photo courtesy of EasyCare, Inc.

Tacking up. Grace and Smurf are ready to head out on the trail. Photo © B. J. McKinney.

CHAPTER THREE

Riding Alone and in Groups

Trail riding can mean many things to different people. It may mean riding down a park trail at the edge of a large city. It can mean a lonely pack trip in the mountains. Perhaps it is a friendly gathering of a few friends to ride around the neighborhood, or on a special outing to a nearby national forest. It can mean riding with a large group on an organized ride such as the Fort Robinson Trail Ride, the Outlaw Trail, or one of the rides sponsored by the Quarter Horse or Paint Horse Associations. It might even mean going on a special organized tour to trail ride on the beaches of California for a week, or some other far-off place. Trail riding opportunities abound for those willing to seek them out. In all of these situations, certain "rules of the trail" should be observed.

RIDING IN GROUPS

One of the most enjoyable parts of trail riding is spending time with friends who have the same interest as you. Riding with a group of other horses can be great, but there are a few things a responsible horse person should keep in mind. These suggestions apply to groups as small as you and just one other person.

The larger the group, the more important it is that you follow this advice.

To prevent surprises and potential accidents, **whenever you want to make a gait change, it is best to announce your intention to your companions.** It is rude, and even dangerous, to increase your speed without first asking if it is all right with everyone else. Chances are your companions' horses will follow, dashing off with very little warning, and an accident could result.

Always ride to the abilities of the least experienced rider or horse. It is terrifying for the novice to find herself with her horse galloping at top speed if she hasn't mastered the trot yet!

If you spot a trail hazard while riding, point it out to your companions in case they don't see it. A simple yell of "broken bottle on the left" could save someone a vet bill. Even better, if possible, stop your horse and fix the problem so every-

One of the most basic rules of group trail riding is that inexperienced riders should never be teamed up with inexperienced horses. At least one of the pair needs to know what he's doing.

Many organized trail rides involve large groups of riders. Photo © Kim Andrews.

one in the future is safe from it. I always appreciate it when I meet other riders on the trail and they warn me about any hazards up ahead, including mountain bikes and loose dogs. If you ride in a public area, remember where the hazards are, find out who to call and give them specifics about the problem, for example, where a tree is down or the trail washed out. If your tone of voice is helpful rather than complaining, you will find that they are grateful for the information and they will remedy the problem as quickly as they can.

A group of horses approaching a street should not cross in single file. Rather, everyone should ride to the edge of the road and when traffic is clear, cross together. This reduces the total amount of time the group of horses is actually on the road. It also prevents a situation I found myself in several times before I wised up. My friend would cross the street first; traffic would appear from nowhere and I would be stranded on the other side until another chance to cross

finally presented itself. This is not a big problem unless your horse is nervous and impatient and wants to get to his companions. Some horses become frantic if they have to stand on the opposite side of the street from the "herd."

While riding alongside a street or roadway, the group should remain in single file. This will keep the horses the farthest away from the traffic and enable cars to pass more safely.

If you are going through a gate on horseback and you must hold it open to get through, do not let it swing into the horse behind you. Find a way to either hold it open—even if it means dismounting—until all the horses are through or allow it to shut before the next horse starts through. Always leave a gate just the way you found it.

On the other hand, **do not try to hold a branch for the rider behind you;** you will have to let it go long before it will do any good. Your friend will get smacked much worse than if you did not try to help at all.

One day I was riding with two other women. At the beginning of the ride one woman, who was on a fractious horse, asked us to tell her ahead of time if we were going to trot or canter so she would be prepared. Both of us turned around and stared at her, surprised she felt she even needed to ask. We assured her we considered it simply common courtesy to warn her of any gait changes. She seemed relieved by our answer. Apparently she had been in many situations where other riders didn't tell her in advance what they were going to do. I know that has happened a few times with me, and it can be quite disconcerting. It is especially bad when I'm riding a green horse and my companions decide to canter off with no warning.

Avoid running up behind another rider, and do not pass because it encourages the horses to race. The bigger the group, the worse the race can become. If possible, try to canter and gallop in single file, and insist that the horses maintain their position in the group. Keep a reasonable distance between horses. Sometimes our horses will get the better of us when we are cantering in a group. If your horse starts closing the gap and is coming up really fast behind another

Everybody should start crossing the road at the same time.

horse, give the other rider a warning. She will appreciate it—I guarantee it.

Any time you plan to ride with one or more people, **choose your companions wisely.** It's great to have company to ride with, but it changes the dynamics of the ride. Always be honest about the experience levels of both you and your horse. If you are on a green-broke horse or you are a novice and all you plan to do is some walking and light trotting, tell your friend. This way nobody's ride will be spoiled and you will not be put into a dangerous situation. The same is true if you are conditioning your horse for an event and plan to trot for the first five miles and canter the next five. Not everyone is interested in that kind of riding. One day while I was riding a youngster, I came upon a woman on a Morgan. I invited her to join me, but told her that I was only going to walk. She said in a determined voice, "No, thank you—today we are going to

While traveling fast, maintain some distance between horses and do not pass the rider ahead. Photo © John Burkett.

A friend of mine moved her Paint mare to a new barn so she would have good trails to ride. She wanted to ride out as soon as possible but didn't know the layout of the trails. A group of retired men in their seventies was going out, and Diane asked if she could join them, thinking it would be a nice, quiet ride. She couldn't have been more wrong. The men were walking quietly along when suddenly they took off at top speed for a long stretch of trail. Of course, the Paint mare followed as best she could. Just as suddenly, the men slammed on the brakes and walked for a while before bursting off into a canter again. They did this off and on for several hours, and Diane was stuck because she didn't know the way back. Later on, she found out that the men, nicknamed "The Wild Boys," rode this way every weekend. A few simple questions and Diane would have had this information before the ride.

canter," and went off in a flash. Later I found out her horse was giving her problems because he had just had several days off and she wanted to take the starch out of him. We would certainly have been mismatched companions on that day! Since then, we have become good friends and have ridden together many times.

Be sure to leave enough space between horses. A full horse length should be the minimum distance you allow. Even horses not known for kicking can surprise you. Keeping your horse far enough away from the horse ahead will also stop your mount from being tempted to nibble on his friend. It is quite inconsiderate to allow your horse to chew on another. Although chewing on other horses can be a form of affection, it can also be an act of aggression. Most of the time if you know

the other horse and rider well, no harm is done, but it does allow your horse to get into a bad habit.

The faster the speed at which you are traveling, the more space there should be between horses. Once I was riding my horse Cruiser, and my boyfriend was riding my other horse, Mingo. We were cantering, and Cruiser got a bit too close to Mingo. Suddenly, Cruiser stumbled. Mingo heard the commotion behind him and slowed down. (Mingo slows down with any excuse.) Cruiser recovered before he hit the ground, but as he was scrambling back to his feet, his front hoof sliced Mingo's hind leg. We were only a few miles away from home, so we hobbled back. It took twelve stitches and two months for Mingo to heal. A little more distance between the horses would have prevented this injury.

While riding in a group, **you are responsible for your horse's behavior**, so it is important that you actively teach him to behave well with other horses. He must allow space around the other horses on all four sides. If he tries to nip another horse, turn his head away and give him a slap. I've found that a slap with a hollow hand that is painless and yet makes a lot of noise is just as effective as a hard slap that inflicts pain. Even better, make a menacing noise and stop the horse with your rein just as he starts to reach over to nip the other horse. Unless he persists with the annoying behavior, this may be all that is necessary. If you don't meet with success, a slap on the shoulder with the whip or reins will reinforce the punishment.

If two horses try to kick at each other, turn their heads together and thoroughly punish them. Some things are just not to be tolerated. Be sure to warn the people you ride with if your horse has a tendency to kick. A red ribbon tied in his tail is helpful to remind anyone approaching from the rear of the danger. I worked with a very docile Quarter Horse mare that only kicked when she was in season and that had an amazing ability to target the other rider's

Horses like to chew on each other if given a chance. Every time we get too close to Cruiser, Ranger can't resist taking a bite. Photo © John Burkett.

leg with each kick. I soon learned to let riders pass us on the trail only if the mare's nose was facing in and her hindquarters well away from the other horses.

Throughout the summer, my local chapter of the Ohio Horse Council sponsors group trail rides in different parts of our park system. Because the groups can be large, a "walk-only" rule is in place. Horses can act crazy when they are with the "herd," and the larger

Don't let behavior like this go unpunished. Photo © John Burkett.

When riding on steep trails, keep at least one horse's length between mounts. Photo © Kim Andrews.

the herd, the worse they behave. A walk-only rule is appropriate for any large group. Most people like it, since they can bring their kids or green horses and know they will be safe. Keep this in mind if you are organizing a large group ride.

RIDING ALONE

Every trail rider will tell you that it is safer to ride with someone else. This is undeniably true. Riding alone is a peaceful, enjoyable experience, but it is definitely riskier than riding in a group. Quite simply, if an accident happens, you have no one to help you.

Some horses are barn sour and dislike going out alone; others are spooky and more inclinded to shy or balk at strange objects when they are alone.

On the other hand, some horses behave much better on their own, making solo riding the safest option. Sometimes a horse just doesn't get along well with other horses and thus would jeopardize the safety of fellow riders, yet the horse is fine by himself. My first horse was like that. If he was with another horse, all he wanted to do was race, particularly on the way home.

Some horses are such dangerous kickers that a rider can't enjoy herself because of her concern for everyone else. Most problems will get better in time with proper handling, but you have to consider your riding companions. There are times when it is safer to ride alone.

Too, sometimes in this hectic, stressful world, you just need to get away. And then it is simply wonderful to ride by yourself. There is no better way to get to know your horse and truly commune with nature. Although I know it is safer to ride with someone and I do enjoy riding with others, I have to admit I cherish my time alone also.

A competent rider should not let the added risk deter her from riding by herself. There have been a number of summers that if I didn't ride by myself, I wouldn't have gone out on the trail more than a handful of times.

The best precaution you can take when riding alone is to **tell someone where you are going and when you plan to return.** In the event that you do not come back at the appropriate time, or if your horse comes back without you, people will know where to look. One friend went on a trail ride without telling anyone where she was going. Her horse got tangled in some old barbed wire and somehow fell. He couldn't get up. Dottie was caught with her leg pinned underneath the horse and was stuck for two hours. She doesn't remember clearly how she got her leg free and the horse untangled, for it was all a nightmare to her. She was gone a long time, and no one knew where to find her. Fortunately, she was able get herself loose, and neither she nor her horse were so badly injured

Trail Courtesy

- Check your gear before you ride. Make sure it is safe and that you have everything you will need, depending upon the weather, terrain, length of ride, and so on.
- Know your limits. Be sure you and your horse are in condition.
- Don't take an unsafe, inexperienced or untrained horse on a group ride. Train first with experienced horses and riders with which you have ridden before.
- Never leave the trailhead until all riders are mounted.
- Never pass on the trail without asking first if it is okay with the rider ahead.
- Never ride away from a dismounted rider on the trail.
- When encountering obstacles such as a bridge, creek, biker, or other hazards, wait until all riders in the group are safely past the obstacle before proceeding.
- Never pass the trail boss.
- Don't let your horse run up on, nuzzle, or scratch on other horses.
- If your horse has a tendency to kick at other horses, tie a ribbon on his tail.
- Always carry out all your trash, and any that other people have left. Protect your right to use the trails.

that they couldn't get back home. This story could easily have had a different, less fortunate ending.

Under all circumstances, **err on the side of safety** by choosing your most cautious option since there will be no one to help you in an emergency. If your choice is to go up a steep, dangerous hill or to ride an extra mile to skirt around it, ride the extra mile. If you intend to venture into unfamiliar territory, get a map of the area and, if possible, check

Sometimes one just needs to get away at the end of a stressful day. Photo © J. C. Leacock Photography.

Many riders recommend carrying a cell phone with important numbers (such as the vet's) programmed in. Be aware, however, that you may move in and out of phone range, depending on the terrain in which you ride.

with local people who may be able to tell you about dangerous areas to avoid.

Generally, you should **be more alert when you are by yourself.** There are only two sets of eyes looking out for you—your horse's and yours. Riding in a group means there are many eyes looking out for hazards in the trail. You're on your own when you are out alone, and all the responsibility for a safe ride falls on you. Please be extra cautious.

New gear should always be tested at home before you hit the trail, particularly if you plan to ride alone. Equipment failure, if it doesn't cause an accident, will at least be a major hindrance. Ten miles away from home is a bad place to find out that your horse just can't stand his new bit because it doesn't fit correctly.

In our area, there is some concern about strangers hanging around in the park. We share our trails with many people and, as with anything that is free to the public, you can encounter some unsavory sorts. If you don't let strangers near your reins, there is little to fear. Many people are frightened of horses and wouldn't dream of getting close enough to do harm. As a precaution, I always carry a whip when I ride alone. If the unthinkable were to happen (and it never has), I could use the whip to defend myself or to jump-start my horse, enabling us to leave the area at top speed. If you are really worried, you might consider carrying pepper spray; this would also help in an encounter with a vicious dog. Just don't spray it into the wind.

CHAPTER FOUR

Riding Through Obstacles

When I first began to trail ride, I thought that you just got on the horse and rode. Since then, I've had horses stumble, sink into deep mud, slip, get tangled in brush, and fall while crossing high water. It wasn't always as easy as I thought it would be. If I were to move to a different part of the country, I'd have to start all over again dealing with the new challenges the different terrain presented.

WHAT IS AN OBSTACLE?

An obstacle can be anything from a puddle to a river bank to a branch on the path. Many things that a hiker or dog walker can easily go through or around become more difficult on a horse. Because of a horse's survival instinct, poor vision, and sheer size, a trip down the trail can become a real adventure. Rides are more challenging, but you also experience the satisfaction of meeting that challenge. It may take a long time for your horse to override his instinct and, without being fearful, move by or through what he perceives as great danger, but time and patience will usually prevail. Don't let it discourage you if it

seems that everything your horse encounters is a major ordeal. Things will get better.

Whenever you see something that you think will bother your horse, slow down and let him look at it. If he gets upset, the problem will be easier to control if you are going slowly. Sometimes an obstacle can simply be given a wide berth; other times the trail will not allow this, and you will have to pass it by closely. In these cases, let your horse pause and take another look; then ask for a few steps. As long as the horse is reacting quietly and reasonably, praise him. If he acts irrationally, don't use praise in an effort to calm him down. He may mistake it as a reward.

When dealing with obstacles, it is important to keep a long-term perspective. Your goal is to help your horse become confident and savvy on the trail, not to force him past this one particular obstacle at whatever the cost. Good riders give their horses the time needed to study the obstacle from as many directions as possible, and they have no qualms about dismounting and leading their horses if necessary.

Mingo, my breeding stock Paint, doesn't like the way this jacket looks in the trees, but I take the time to show it to him. A horse will notice anything that seems out of place. Photo by Kevin Curry.

If your horse trusts you, it is sometimes safer to lead him through scary situations. He will follow if you go first.

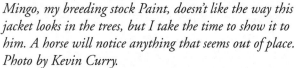

Horses are prey animals, and they view humans are predators. Because of this, the two animals view the world in very different ways, both literally and figuratively. The horse has eyes on the outside of his head, giving him excellent peripheral but limited binocular vision. When encountering an unknown object, generally his immediate instinct is to flee—this is basic survival behavior. He often will need to study an object from many angles before he can accept it as safe. Punishing him or threatening him will only scare him more. Your job is to get the horse to accept you not simply as a member of his herd, but as the leader of that herd. That way, he can relax and rely on your judgment about surrounding dangers. He will still get frightened at times, but he can, under your control, learn to modify his behavior. The process takes time, but the results are well worth it.

When riding in a group, the bravest, boldest horse should always go first. Trying to get the more fearful horse to go first may make the other horses scared as well. Depending on the horse, you may have more success by getting off and leading him past the obstacle. Use your judgment here. Every horse is different. A horse that trusts his rider may decide that if she goes first, it is safe for him to follow. However, a rider has less control leading than riding, and a terrified horse may pull and try to get away. If this happens, try to spin him by pulling on the closest rein until he stops. Typically, he will stop when he is facing the object. Ask him to walk by it one step at a time, and keep his head turned toward the object. Whether leading or riding, once you are past the object, praise your horse profusely. I always reach down and rub my mount's neck with both hands. My horses really seem to like that.

Trails available throughout the country vary greatly, ranging from quiet country lanes to beaches, deserts and mountains. Regardless of where you ride, one thing is always required. Even in familiar areas, riders must be completely aware of their surroundings. An alert rider will notice glass on the path or a new groundhog hole before it is too late.

Fortunately, you are not alone in your vigilance. Horses have excellent memories and will memorize the trails coming and going in all weather and at all times of the day, much like the steamboat captains in the days before technology replaced the skill of the navigator. These men had to know every foot of the rivers they traveled in every season and at every depth, and they were continually alert for the slightest changes that would affect their passage.

Horses are equally vigilant. They always notice a change in their environment. This is how wild horses survive, and our domestic horses haven't lost the skill. If a rider pays attention to her mount, he will point out changes and possible dangers. Keep in mind, though, that it is up to you make the final decision about whether it is safe to continue or not. At the same time, do not doubt your horse's ability to determine the safest route. After all, his business is survival.

The faster you ride, the more important vigilance becomes. Alternate between looking in the immediate vicinity and looking out to the distance. The objective is to be able to make decisions as early as possible, allowing you to slow down before arriving at the new obstacle or to choose the correct maneuver around a branch or slick puddle. Naturally, if the ground is very rough, you will not be traveling fast. Your horse should be allowed to walk and pick his way through bad areas. If there is any

The faster you ride the more important it becomes to be watchful.

doubt as to the safety of the trail, don't risk an accident by trying to negotiate it.

DIFFICULT FOOTING

Always look ahead for any difficult footing. This may include mud, rocks or ice. By being observant, you should be able to slow down to a walk before you reach it. A little mud can be trotted or cantered through as long as you use caution and keep your speed at a safe pace. Really deep mud should be walked through—not only does it upset a lot of horses, it can bow a tendon or pull off a shoe. Ice should be avoided at all costs.

Occasionally, you may find yourself on a patch of ice by accident. Ask your horse to stop, then dismount and slowly lead him off the ice. He will do better without you on his back, and you won't be hurt if he should fall. Be careful not to fall yourself. Once I fell on ice and hit both knees so hard I couldn't walk. Cruiser made it to the other side of the

PREPARE IN ADVANCE

Any horse that you plan to take on trail rides should be introduced to obstacles first at home in the safety of a round pen or arena. Make a mud puddle and teach your horse to walk through it. You can make a water box to simulate a stream by setting four two by six by ten foot two by four boards on edge to form a square. Place a blue tarp over the boards and fill the inside of the frame with water. It may take some time for your horse to learn to walk across this.

You can create other obstacles at home as well. Make a small bridge from a heavy shipping pallet or by laying a sheet of plywood on the ground. Ask your horse to walk over this, or over poles, logs, or a tarpoline lying flat on the ground. Hang flags on the fence, or a yellow slicker. Test your horse's response to saddle bags or water bottle holders in the arena; not on the trail. Teach your horse to maneuver around and through barrels and poles. Create a narrow passageway by placing a pole or a couple of barrels next to a fence and walking him through it. Make sure you can back your horse as well as ride forward through the obstacles. You never know when you might need to back out of a narrow spot because the trail is blocked for some reason.

On the trail an inexperienced horse may balk at a puddle, spook at a piece of trash blowing in the wind, or shy away from a roadside mailbox and into the path of traffic. He may be terrified by a biker, a hiker with a backpack, or an unfamiliar animal. Make sure he has experienced as many of these situations either at home or in the company of a few other experienced horses and riders before you venture out on a lengthy ride. Otherwise, you could have a long walk home, with or without your horse!

ice patch and waited for me. I crawled over the ice to get to him, and he stood quietly as I climbed up his body and leaned on him. He then slowly walked me to the barn. That day, I realized first-hand how bad ice could be.

Rocky ground should be covered at a walk. Even small rocks and gravel can bother a horse's feet, so be kind and allow your horse to pick his own way through. In all cases of difficult footing, the principal rule is that you use your common sense.

My sister was riding Cruiser over a hill that he must have been on at least a hundred times before and came upon a bright blue bucket close to the trail. Cruiser was quite upset—he know the bucket hadn't been there before. He did his snorting routine and made a big fuss, but his rider firmly insisted he pass it. The very next day I rode Cruiser past the same bucket again, unaware of what had happened. He merely paused, pointed it out to me and continued on once he knew I wasn't worried. He never looked at the bucket again; it became part of the scenery. I'm sure that if someone were to move it to the other side of the trail, we would go through the whole routine again.

HILLS

Hills present an obstacle for some horses while others just take them in stride. Whether out of fear or awkwardness, horses may stall out or rush off while going up or down a hill. They are not born with the ability to traverse hills well; this must be learned. Since few trails are totally without hills, it is important that a horse acquires the skill to handle them. It is even more difficult with a rider aboard. Green horses are still trying to figure out how to carry a rider, let alone how to carry that rider up or down a steep hill. They often alternate between rushing and freezing up and only taking a step or two at a time. Much patience is necessary with these inexperienced horses. If your horse freezes, it may help to get off and lead him. He is probably unsure of himself and watching you go first will give him the confidence to continue. At the same time, you are relieving him of the burden of having you on his back.

The horse that rushes up or down a hill needs to be slowed down gently. It's not a good idea to lead horses that rush, because they tend to go too fast for a person on foot to lead safely. It's better just to ride it out. The first few hills that I took Cruiser down when he was three years old were quite challenging. He simply couldn't coordinate his legs to stay at a walk. By the time he reached the bottom, we were at a fast trot—once we even ended up cantering. I just kept turning him around, and back we would go to try again. I didn't quit until he showed some improvement. It took about a half dozen rides like this before he could walk down a hill. Knowing that in this case it was a coordination problem and not a behavior problem helped me keep my patience.

Always walk when on gravel.

Rushing up or down a hill is not always a question of coordination. Some horses simply want to be in control. When I was a young girl, the first time I rode down a steep hill my horse, Brandy, started to trot halfway down. My aunt was riding with me and said not to worry, she rode him down this hill on a regular basis and Brandy wouldn't go any faster. Just as she said that, he began to canter. He knew exactly what he was doing: I was a young, inexperienced rider, and he was going to take me for a ride. Years later, my aunt gave me this same horse. Even then it took a lot of patience on my part to slow him down, but because I was an older and more confident rider, he never tried to run down a hill again. Going uphill was a different matter–eventually, however, he would even do that quietly.

When traveling uphill, an inexperienced horse will try to pull himself up with his forelegs instead of bringing his hind legs well under him. A horse can be taught to use his hind legs more

Never let your horse rush up or down a hill. Photo © K. S. Swigart.

efficiently by tapping him lightly with a whip in the middle of the rump just as he's stepping underneath himself to encourage him to step farther. When he understands, be sure to praise him profusely. Soon he will have developed the muscles necessary and will use this method of hill climbing all the time on his own because it will be easier for him. The strong hindquarter muscles also are necessary for controlled descent on steep hills.

Do not restrict your horse's head by strong contact with the reins. He needs his head and neck to help with balance.

Most advice about traveling on a hill will tell you to lean forward or back. In truth, your position doesn't change at all from when you are riding on the flat ground. Rather, your horse's position changes underneath you. It will just appear that you lean forward as you go up and backward as you go down. It might help to think of your back as a fence post stuck in the ground on the hill. The fence post is straight; the hill is slanted. With this posture, you ride well balanced and are far less likely to interfere

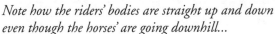

Note how the riders' bodies are straight up and down even though the horses' are going downhill...

...or uphill. Photos © Kim Andrews.

with your horse. If you are unsure about your position, compare your body to straight trees growing on the hill near you.

On steep hills you can help your horse to balance by "walking" with your feet in the stirrups. As your horse's left foreleg is on the ground, rest your weight in the left stirrup. Then, as his right foreleg lifts and moves forward, walk your right leg slightly forward and rest your weight on that side as his right fore is planted on the trail.

A good rule of thumb is not to ride your horse up or down a hill that is so steep that, if you were climbing it on foot, you would need to use your hands on the hill for balance. If you must go up a very steep hill, you can give your horse a break by leading him. (This will also warm you up on a cold winter ride.) Don't get in front of your horse, because he may unintentionally go too fast and knock you over. At the very least, he may step on the back of your heels, which can be quite painful. It is safest to stay at his side.

Some endurance riders will "tail" a horse up a hill, that is, will let a horse go up a hill on his own while the rider grabs his tail to help pull her up. This isn't the safest thing to do unless you take the time to train your horse for it. It also isn't necessary in a noncompetitive situation.

When riding in a group, never resume faster speeds at the bottom of the hill until everyone is down. All the horses will naturally want to follow yours at the same speed, and it could be disastrous! Cruiser walks down hills so fast that I must always stop at the bottom and wait for my companions to catch up with us. Sometimes I even stop halfway down because we get too far ahead. I routinely turn my head to check on my companions. I always insist that he walk, and since Cruiser never stumbles, I allow him to go down at his most comfortable speed. We are careful that the accompanying horses do

Some horses find zigzagging down a hill easier. Photo by Kevin Curry.

JUMPS

It is very handy and fun to have a horse that is willing to jump a log on the trail. Your horse may already have the training to do a little jumping, but before you go leaping over anything that comes in your path, you need to check it out. Slow to a walk when you come up to a log for the first time, and approach it quietly to get a good look at it. By checking the jump first, you might prevent a mishap. ("Look before you leap" has concrete application here.) Do not canter or trot to the log and suddenly stop—this may introduce to your horse the idea of refusing to take a jump.

Sometimes you will find the ground very slippery in the takeoff or landing area. Other times, you will discover branches sticking out of the log that would have interfered with your jump. If you can clear them away and make the jump safe, by all means, do so. This not only makes a safe jump for you, but it will help anyone else who comes along, particularly someone who isn't as cautious as you. Your inspection may also reveal that the jump is greater than your abilities or your horse's experience. At that point, start looking for a way to get around it.

After you have determined a log is safe to jump, turn your horse around, move back the necessary distance for your horse to approach the jump, and go for it. Even if you have jumped this log before and don't feel you need to check it out first, be alert as you canter towards it. Prepare yourself for a surprise.

You should not jump even a safe log if your horse is physically unable to due to a previous injury or if he is less than four years old. A young horse needs to mature before he can take the impact of jumping.

not get excited and try to trot to catch up with us. If we anticipate any problems, we will either let the other horses go down the hill first, giving them a big head start, or we will stop partway down the hill to let them catch up.

Some horses learn to go up or down a wide path on a steep hill in a zigzag fashion. By doing this, each step is less steep than if he went straight. Don't accuse your horse of being balky if he does this—he's actually being smart. If your horse hasn't figured out on his own how to zigzag, you can ask him to try it. This may become his preferred method of travel on hills. He may, however, feel more comfortable going straight if he doesn't have very good balance, coordination or flexibility. The more you work him out on the trails, the more these traits will improve. It's just one more way trail riding will help make your horse a better mount in all aspects of his life.

It's a good idea to spend some time in the arena with your horse to get him accustomed to jumping if he has never been jumped before. Even a person who rides Western may want to do this. Small jumps are quite reasonable in a Western saddle, and they are often included in Western trail classes. Whole books have been written on teaching your horse to jump, but if you only want to pop over the occasional log on the trail, you do not need to train him as intensely as if your destination is the show ring.

You are not actually teaching the horse how to jump; he already knows this. You are merely helping him learn to size up the jump and to approach it so he will take off at a good spot and jump with confidence. To force a horse to jump on a trail ride when he has had little experience with jumping can shake his trust in you and disillusion him about trail riding.

A great way to start your jumping training is simply to trot over poles on the ground. After some practice, you'll find that your horse seems very comfortable doing this. It also builds up his confidence for trotting over small logs that you may find on the trail.

Now it's time to try a small jump. Put two poles side by side and raise one end up on each side. They will form a "V" and the center will be the lowest part. This will be your first jump. The low spot will encourage him to aim for the center of the jump. Make sure the jump is low enough that he can still trot over it without jumping. Trot over it a few times; then canter to it. When you canter, be prepared for him to jump higher than he needs to. A horse must learn to determine the height of a jump, and sometimes it may take a while for him to figure out how to do this. On trail, always be prepared for your horse

Look before you leap.

Even when you think you know an obstacle well, it is important to watch for something unexpected. I had been jumping a fairly good-sized obstacle made of two logs side by side for several weeks. But one day, as I cantered up to the logs, I noticed someone had placed a very small log in front that lengthened the jump. This didn't worry me too much. Right as I was about to take off, though, I was able to see that a fourth log had also been added to the far side of the jump, making it much wider than I had ever jumped before. There wasn't anything I could do at that point but jump. We did just fine since I had been prepared for a change and was able to adjust to the new situation.

to overjump if he misjudges the height. The jump may appear more formidable in his eyes than it really is.

Don't overdo it while schooling your horse for jumping. You don't want to make him bored or sore. It should be

Ellen demonstrates on Ranger how your spine should be perpendicular to the ground when traveling up or down hill. Note the logs that have been pushed aside on this trail.

The park system I ride in has very well-maintained trails, and the crews quickly remove logs when they are reported to them. I am always disappointed when the good jumping logs are removed. I even go so far as to ask people not to report these logs so I can keep jumping them for a few weeks. Eventually, the park always finds out and cleans them up. On the other hand, I really appreciate it when they take away the unsafe logs that I must find a way to get around. Here, as elsewhere, something bad usually also has some good.

something he enjoys or at least takes in stride. Gradually raise the jump until it is the height of the largest log you will attempt to jump on the trail. You can also adjust the jump to make it wider. Up to this point, your jumps should have been made so they would fall apart when they are hit. Now, if you can, bring some logs into the arena to jump. (Lighter weight, rotten logs are easier to move and do the job just as well as their heavier counterparts.) A log not only looks different, it is solid. Your horse will learn to take logs seriously after he brushes his hooves against them a few times.

Soon you will be ready to jump logs out on the trail. If you are lucky, you will find a few good ones that you can practice on. Look for small logs that go across the entire trail and thus don't allow your horse to dash around them. Praise your horse when he does well, and before you know it, both of you will be

jumping with happy confidence. Horses seem to genuinely enjoy jumping out on trail. It's like a game to them.

DOGS

Occasionally, a loose dog appears on the scene. As tough and aggressive as a dog may seem, he will usually back off if you turn your horse to face him. If you retreat, chances are very good that the dog will chase you. Most dogs will chase anything that runs away from them. One day as I was riding home, a young Dachshund confidently came running up to us head-on. We just stopped and looked at him. When he was a dozen feet away, he stopped, spun around and then ran straight away from us. I don't think he ventured too far away from his owners for a long time after that. This was a fairly normal dog reaction.

Still, use caution. Every now and then, there is an exception to the rule. My friend Judy was out riding when a dog jumped at her horse's hindquarters. The horse reared and Judy fell off. The dog then attacked her face—he had been encouraged to be vicious by his owner. Thank goodness an incident like this is far from typical.

If a loose dog approaches you, turn your horse towards him and stop. The dog will probably leave you alone. Some dogs will try to circle your horse. Just keep turning so your horse is always facing the dog. If the dog gets behind you, he may cause your horse to bolt forward or to kick out. Actually, the dog is at more risk in these situations than the horse. Tell the owner, if there is one, that your horse may kick if the dog goes behind you, and most likely you will find that the dog is speedily caught up. Any horse might kick if he is startled, and a horse's kick can kill a dog.

While it is true that in most places dogs are required to be leashed, we are still responsible for our horse's behavior. If a loose dog or even one on a leash startles a horse, it is not the dog owner's fault the horse got frightened. We must take the time to accustom our horses to dogs. Fortunately, most horses are used to being around dogs, for few stables lack them. If your horse is not used to them, borrow a friend's dog and carefully introduce them to each other. The best kind of dog to use is one already familiar with horses. When performing the introduction, remember that the dog is vulnerable not only to kicks from the horse's hindquarters, but also to strikes from the forelegs.

Cruiser just loves dogs, and we have taken the time to "horse-break" a number of dogs for our friend, Ann. Ann in turn uses her dogs to "dog-break" the horses she meets. We all share the same trails, so why not make them better for everyone, whether equine, canine or human?

BIKES

When I first started trail riding years ago, I seldom encountered bikes on the trail. When I did, they terrified my horse. Bikes are very quiet and, from a horse's point of view, they move in an unnatural way. Now, with the popularity of mountain bikes, they are very common. The only good thing about that is that we have plenty of opportunities to accustom our horses to bikes.

Unlike Cruiser, my horse Mingo doesn't like dogs at all. Once two dogs dashed out of a car and ran right to his heels. I was leading him through a parking lot at the time, so it was very hard for me to turn him quickly to face the dogs. (Had I been riding him, this would have been fairly easy.) He kicked out and missed. That was enough to scare one of the dogs, but the other one ran right back to his heels. This time, Mingo was able to make contact and tossed the dog twenty feet away. Happily, the dog was unhurt. The owners learned a valuable lesson and were very apologetic. I've taken advantage of the situation. From that day on I've told everyone I meet with a loose dog that Mingo kicks dogs. They quickly get their dogs under control. I'm glad to say he hasn't kicked a dog since, but I still don't trust him with a dog close to his heels.

A horse with a bad fear should be desensitized at home. Find a friend with a bike and bring it out to your stable. Start by putting the bike on its kickstand and leading your horse to it. Surprisingly, to some horses an immobile bike is more frightening than a moving one. Don't rush your horse; let him visit the bike at his own pace. Horses are naturally curious, so eventually he will want to get a closer look. Praise him with every step forward. It is important for your horse to view it from straight on, from his left side, from his right side and from behind. A horse may be very calm looking at an obstacle from one side but not the other, since he doesn't have a good connection between the left and right halves of his brain. Usually, the whole procedure must be repeated from scratch when he sees it from the opposite side.

While you are working on immobile bikes, lay the bike on its side and start the process all over. Owners frequently drop their bikes by the side of the trail while they explore the area on foot, and horses just don't know what to make of it.

Once your horse is accustomed to a stationary bike, it is time to teach him that a moving bike is similarly harmless. Have an assistant ride the bike in circles or back and forth. Begin with the assistant at a distance, and gradually bring your horse closer and closer, just as you did with the standing bike. Carry on a conversation with the biker so your horse will know there's a human involved. Praise the horse whenever he is quiet. If he should get very nervous and uptight and show no signs of improving, quit for the day and try again another time. Eventually, add more and more potentially frightening acts, such as the biker approaching from behind, skidding to a stop and riding circles around your horse. Again, praising your horse when he does well is the key to success.

A typical horse that isn't already terrified of bikes can be worked with them out on the trail the same as any other obstacle. Your job is to stay alert so that a bike doesn't catch you or your horse by surprise. As a bike approaches you, stop your horse, face the bike and let it pass. Even better, ask the biker to stop his bike and let you pass. This is the absolute safest thing a biker can do, both for you and himself, when he sees a horse. Praise the bike rider if he stops on his own to encourage him to do it in the future. (Positive reinforcement works with people as well as it does with horses.) You may want to trot after the bike for a little way to show your horse it will run away from him. Most horses lose their fear of anything they can be coaxed to chase.

Although where I ride, bike riders are not allowed on the trails, I have given up telling them so. Instead, I spend my time politely asking them to stop and let us pass, and then thanking them profusely for their cooperation. I've found educating bikers to be more effective than lecturing them. They take the advice and use it. On the worst stretch of trail for bikes that I ride on, nearly all the bike riders are now stopping their bikes well ahead of us and letting us pass. I never fail to thank them. The rangers can enforce the rules; I just plan to teach the bike riders how to co-exist with us. In the meantime, I am working to have more signs posted in our area and to get the rangers to patrol them more often.

Many places allow horses and bikes to share the same trails. In these areas, education is even more important so we can share the trails in peace and safety.

Motor bikes can be another story altogether. They can appear noisily out of nowhere, make sudden, loud pops or roars and move so fast that a horse hardly sees them, If you plan to ride where off-road bikers may travel, be sure your horse has met these vehicles before in flat, open terrain and is not afraid of them. As with a regular bike, it is best to stop and turn your horse toward the motor bike.

STEPS

Now and then, you may encounter steps on the trail. Horses are very capable of going up or down steps, but it takes a while for them to become competent at it. Until he has had a lot of experience on them, it will be best for you to get off and lead your horse up or down the steps. Let him take his time and praise him as he goes to give him encouragement. Make sure that you are in a safe position while leading him in case he should stumble or suddenly decide to dart forward.

MUD HOLES

Deep mud can be a serious problem. If the ground on the trail looks at all suspicious, stay away from it. There is no way of knowing how deep the mud is, what might be lying within the hole, or whether the ground is level or rutted under the mud. Be careful—even if the hole isn't wide, it can be very deep. One woman stepped into a narrow mud hole and she later told me that it was like stepping off a cliff when her horse suddenly went down to his knees. So play it safe and go around the hole or walk on the edges. Be particularly wary of mud holes in areas where dirt bikes and ATVs share the trails.

Sometimes the unexpected happens and you find yourself mired in the mud. Stay calm. Never forget that your horse is sure to panic if you don't hold yourself together. Give your horse his head, lean forward and urge him to go straight ahead. Jennifer was riding her Quarter Horse, Martins Lullabye, with some friends. Her horse was in the lead, and everyone was taken by surprise when she sunk in a mud/clay mixture halfway up her stirrup leathers. There was absolutely no indication at all that there was a mud hole; it looked no different than the solid ground surrounding it. Fortunately, Jennifer was encouraged to stay calm and urge her horse forward by her "old timer" trail riding partners. In five good leaps, they made it to the other side unscathed.

Sometimes you can safely turn your horse if the mud isn't too deep, and you fear that the mud hole might be too wide to cross to the other side. Go slowly and take one step at a time. It is harder to turn than to go straight forward. It is best to stay in the saddle until your horse is on solid ground. If you dismount and also get stuck in the mud, there is no way for you to quickly get out of your horse's way if he should panic and start thrashing around. Upon reaching safety, dismount and check the horse for injury. You should also make sure he didn't lose any shoes. Sometimes deep mud will pull them right off.

In some areas the edges of harmless looking streams or ponds may contain "quicksand," which is a mixture of clay and sand that can give way without warning and literally suck you and your horse deeper and deeper into the mire. If you ride in areas where quicksand is known to occur, check the footing near streams and ponds very carefully before leading your horse out to them. If your horse begins to sink, try to get his forelegs over a log or onto a solid rock. Prevent him from thrashing. If you cannot free him in a short time, get help. Quicksand can literally swallow up a thrashing animal before they can be pulled out.

When you first approach a puddle, be prepared for your horse to either try to go around it or jump it. If you think he may jump, and if the landing looks safe, stay well back of the horse ahead of you. Allow plenty of room for a safe landing. Keep going back and forth over small streams or puddles, asking your horse to walk until he will approach slowly and cross without breaking stride. If, on the other hand, you cannot get him to cross at all, dismount and try standing at the edge of the puddle and "driving" him forward over it. Eventually he should learn to cross without hesitation.

Practice crossing small wooden bridges anytime you can. You will likely encounter many different types of bridges on the trail. Photo © Lourie Ann Zipf.

CHAPTER FIVE

Riding in Traffic

Few people today have the luxury of being able to ride in fields or unpopulated trails. If you want to get out the the arena, you may have to ride at least a short way on a busy roadway. Don't attempt this alone the first time unless you know that your horse has been desensitized to the type of traffic you are likely to encounter. In rural areas this can include many different types of large equipment. On major highways you could encounter a myriad of vehicles, from semi trucks to cement mixers, pickups with trailers, convertibles or motorbikes. On dual-purpose trails or back-country roads expect to meet atv's, jeeps, and other unusual vehicles. While you probably can't arrange for your horse to encounter every type of vehicle at home, expose him to as many as possible before venturing onto the highway.

ROADS

The legal way to ride alongside a road is with the direction of traffic, just as you would on a bicycle. If the road has a very narrow berm on that side or the visibility is better on the other side, it is probably safer to cross over. Safety should always be your first concern. I don't think any policeman would give you a ticket for riding on the wrong side of the road if you gave him an explanation that showed you were only doing it to be safe. If you can travel on the correct side of the road, though, please do. It is easier for the automobiles to pass if you are traveling in the same direction that they are.

Sometimes it is necessary to ride on pavement. Be extra careful if your horse's shoes are worn. He will have a tendency to slip, particularly on slopes. You may even want to dismount and allow him to step carefully without your interference. If he does slip, he may be able to regain his balance better without you on his back. Also, if the unthinkable happens and he falls, you will be unharmed. Avoid going any faster than a walk on the pavement because the impact is extremely bad for your horse's legs and the risk for slipping increases. Save the trotting and cantering for the trails where it is safer.

Be aware of the traffic all around you. Since it's not practical to look behind you every ten seconds, learn to listen carefully for cars. It may be that your horse is good with cars, but is nervous around motorcycles or trucks. By listening, you can be prepared for a

Always walk on pavement to save your horse's feet and joints. Photo by Ellen Daly.

When riding along highways, stay single file and ride in the same direction as the traffic. Photo © Carien Schippers.

problem and turn your horse to see the oncoming vehicle.

Always follow the rules of the road. Stop at stop signs and lights, cross in crosswalks where available, and respect the other people on the road.

I like to teach my horses to stop at an intersection and wait for a few moments, even if there are no cars coming towards us. This gets them in the habit of stopping there. There is nothing more annoying and dangerous than a horse that doesn't want to stop and wait for a car to pass. Horses are at their worst when on their way home, so be especially cautious at those times. Getting your horse into a routine of stopping helps ensure that he will be cooperative even then.

If your horse refuses to stop at a street, pull his head to the side and force him into a circle to avoid stepping on the road. It may not look pretty, but it will keep your horse where he belongs. If he won't settle down, face away from the road until it is safe to cross. When

Stop at all intersections and wait for the cars to pass.

If your horse won't stop at a street, pull his head around and circle him away from the road.

the coast is clear, turn him back to the road and ask for a proper stop. Keep repeating this exercise until the horse finally gets it right. As a reward, praise him; then continue on your way. Stopping the circling game is actually quite a reward in itself—horses hate to circle.

Some horses seem to understand they are supposed to stop and wait for a single car to go by before crossing, but they don't grasp the larger concept that they are supposed to wait for all the cars to pass. In areas where there isn't much traffic, the horses get into a routine. As soon as the first car passes, they try to step out into the road, even though another car might be heading straight for them. Being aware that your horse might try this can help you prevent an accident.

BRIDGES

Bridges offer another big challenge. Not only do they look scary, they often sound different, which can ratchet up a horse's fear another notch. The presence or the absence of a railing can make your horse uneasy, too. The situation is worse if there is a lot of traffic on the road. If your horse has been taught to lead well, and he trusts you, the best choice may be to lead him—it's a judgment call on your part. In theory, you will have more control riding the horse since you can control the front half with the reins and the back half with your legs, but he may simply be less afraid if he sees you walking over the bridge with him.

You will be safer on the ground because you have less risk of falling. I say "less risk" instead of "no risk" because you still can be stepped on or knocked

OTHER ROAD HAZARDS

One of the biggest problems you can have when riding in traffic is "information overload" when your horse encounters not only vehicles on the roadway but simultaneous distractions from other frightening sights and sounds. These can include but are not limited to:

• Diesel smoke or strong exhaust fumes
• Highway signs or signs on buildings along the roadway
• Flags of any type: an American flag on a pole; flags around a used car lot, flags on a store
• Balloons, often used by places of business to draw attention, or by residents marking their driveways for a special event
• Backfiring vehicles; kids tossing firecrackers; loud construction noises, etc.
• Road construction signs, cones, and flagmen
• Kids or dogs running along the road
• Horses or cattle running in a pasture beside the road
• Road graders, street sweepers, garbage trucks, trains and the like

Any time you ride on or beside a road, keep your eyes and ears open in all directions. If you aren't comfortable with how your horse may react, dismount and turn him to face the object of his fear.

If traffic is on one side and the scary object on the other side you can either wait for traffic to pass, try to find a way around, or stop or circle your horse until a better opportunity opens up. When a horse experiences frightening objects on both sides, he may react as if he were encountering a large predator and start to flee in the opposite direction. He may feel he is about to be trapped. Try not to put yourself or your horse in this type of situation by always being alert and looking ahead, behind, and to both sides of the road.

This is Mingo's first trip across a bridge, and he is a little uneasy about the railing. I'm using my leg to keep him as close to the edge as possible. Photo by Kevin Curry.

over by a frightened horse. At least if you are leading, the distance isn't as far to fall, and you are not likely to fall off the side of the bridge. If you happen to be traveling with a bridge-safe companion, position him between your horse and the traffic. Your horse will feel safer. After a few times going over the bridge, he will probably be just fine.

FEAR OF TRAFFIC

Some fortunate people living in the outskirts of civilization may be able to ride without having to concern themselves with traffic. The majority of us, however, encounter it quite often—in some cases, every time we ride. Training a horse to be quiet around traffic is a combination of desensitization and getting him to trust your judgment. In time, most horses can become as well behaved in traffic as a city police horse.

How badly your horse behaves with traffic will tell you where to start your training program. Some horses hardly flinch at cars. My Paint colt spent many short training sessions standing at the end of the stable driveway watching cars go by. When it was necessary to move to a new barn down the street a few months later, he hardly noticed the cars, though he was less than a year old. His older companion, a horse with a lot of exposure to traffic, danced around several times. Each horse is different.

If you are lucky, you will have access to a pasture near a road where you can turn your horse out to graze. It will be even better if there are other horses to show him that cars are no big deal. Horses can become desensitized to trains in this way, also. Don't think of the use of the pasture as a cure, but as an introduction. If you don't have access to such a pasture, move on to another tactic.

You can begin to get the horse accustomed to the different sound and feel of a bridge at home in your arena. Build your training bridge by screwing a sheet of three-quarter-inch plywood to a two-by-four frame. Use cross pieces underneath to give support and strength. As you walk your horse across this "bridge," he will experience the changes in footing and sound that can be frightening. He will have time to get used to these before he is exposed to the additional elements of an actual bridge, including a railing and either traffic or water moving underneath.

It's said that tape recording traffic noises and playing them to your horse helps, but I've never talked to anyone who has actually tried this. I'm sure it wouldn't do any harm, and since there is reason to believe it's beneficial, the technique is certainly worth a try. Probably the best time to play the tape is while your horse is eating, thus giving him good positive reinforcement.

For safety, do your early traffic training on foot. Gloves are recommended to prevent rope burns. A thick cotton rope provides a better grip than a thin nylon or leather lead. Narrow lead ropes can slip through your hands and leave horrible wounds—I have the scars to prove it. Tying a couple of knots in strategic places in the rope will give you an even better grip. No matter how often you may have heard it, this valuable advice always bears repeating: Never loop the lead around your hand or fingers. Periodically check to make sure your hands are safe. I've been knocked over and dragged, but because I'm always careful, I have never gotten worse than wet and muddy. (For some reason, this never happens in a dry place!)

Now that you have your gloves and knotted lead rope, you can begin the actual training. Show your horse a parked car, and let him walk around and explore it. He may be apprehensive about approaching it, so give him time to observe it from a distance. Advance towards the car a step or two at a time, allowing him to pause and think. This also gives you a chance to praise him when he is good. You must set a good example by remaining calm and breathing regularly. I guarantee he will be watching for your reaction. Be careful when you get close to the car. One horse I had was leery of parked automobiles; however, when he finally got close enough, he tried to take a bite out of one.

Once your horse is comfortable with parked cars, let a friend start the car so your horse can get used to an engine running. After a while, your assistant should gun the motor a few times to accustom the horse to the changing sounds. Frequently while I am riding near a road, a car will slow down to look at us and then, just as it passes, the driver will floor the gas pedal and roar away. It is important for your horse to get used to these abrupt changes.

Only when your horse is fine with the noisy parked car, should you have the car go into motion. For the first few lessons, it is best to work in a tightly controlled environment with a driver who will do exactly what you say. Allow your horse to watch the car go up and down the driveway, making sure he sees it from both sides of his head. The hardest part for the horse will be when a car approaches from behind, so practice that many times before you actually go out on the streets. The lessons will go faster if, the first few times, you have a second assistant with a traffic-safe horse showing your horse that this is a normal situation and there is nothing to worry about. Your horse also needs to do this

lesson solo, though, before you take him into a live traffic situation.

Introduce a honking horn the same way as the noisy car. People seem to enjoy honking at horses, and it's a real pleasure to have a horse that doesn't even flinch when it happens. I get a personal sense of satisfaction in denying the obnoxious driver the pleasure of startling my horse. Unfortunately, sometimes I get startled myself. Work on honking horns until your horse can stand quietly when a car right next to him honks as well as when a car comes up from behind and blows the horn just upon reaching him. Praise him profusely when he is good, of course.

The next step in your traffic training is to work in a roadside field or any place where there is some space between you and the traffic. You should have ample room to maneuver if your horse is startled. Let him watch the traffic straight on until he is relaxed. Then lead him back and forth along the road (but not on it) so he gets used to the cars coming from the front and the rear. Again work from both his left and right sides. He should adjust to the average car fairly quickly, but that doesn't mean the occasional bus, truck, air horn or bad exhaust system won't scare him. The worst of all is a snowplow in use! The mere thought of it makes me cringe. As an extra scary vehicle comes towards you, have your horse face it, watch it pass and follow it. A horse learns to not be afraid of anything he can chase. In time, as he improves, you can repeat all of this while mounted.

As his confidence increases, introduce your horse to walking on a quiet road. Once again, if you have a willing friend with a traffic-safe horse, ask them to join you. Either have your friend ride in front so you can follow or, if there is room, have her ride next

You never know what you will find on the trail. Take the time and use the opportunities that present themselves to continue your horse's training.

to you, between your horse and the cars. The better your horse gets, the more difficult traffic situations you should test him on.

Of course, you have to work with the environment that is available to you. I once rode with a woman who had owned an Arab gelding from the time he was two. She told me how she originally kept him on a quiet, rural dead-end street. She literally had to wait for hours for a car to appear. Her horse never experienced real traffic until she moved him to a stable closer to her home. That's where I met her. I only got to trail ride with her one time, and that was when she first started to ride him around traffic. To say her horse was nervous was a huge understatement. She was grateful to have me with her, for her horse was

fine as long as I rode between him and the cars. His training had just been postponed to a time when there was traffic available.

A friend with a motorcycle willing to help you with desensitization is also a great asset. Most horses are more afraid of motorcycles than cars. Teach the lesson in the same way you did with the car.

How long this whole process will take depends on your horse's personality and whether he has a naturally skittish nature, has had a bad experience, or simply because he has never been exposed to traffic. Be patient. At each stage, wait for your horse's body language to tell you he is comfortable before you move on to the next stage. As always, praise, praise and praise.

Don't be envious of the people who have dead-quiet traffic horses. I have a friend who, with her sister, adopted two police horses retired from a big city. The women were certain their new horses would be spook-free. The horses were—as long as they were on a street. Instead, they were afraid of fields and tall grass since it had been so long since they had seen them. Another woman I know has an Arabian stallion that is so unafraid of traffic she has to be very diligent to keep him from stepping into oncoming cars. Each horse has his own set of problems.

CHAPTER SIX

Crossing Water

Many people have to cross creeks or rivers where they ride. The area in which I currently ride follows a river that must be crossed many times. The advantage of riding close to a river is that the horses always have a source of water nearby to prevent dehydration. The river also helps cool the horses on hot days, and it teaches them to cross water willingly. People who ride where there is no water to cross sometimes get anxious whenever they plan a ride where they will encounter it.

The disadvantage to riding by a river is that crossing it can be difficult and even dangerous. I board my horse in an area where the first crossing is only five minutes from the barn, so if the river is raging or icy, we don't get much of a ride. Normally the water level is only one to two feet deep; a heavy rain can cause it to rise to six to eight feet. The current is very strong in that area and the bottom is uneven. Horses have lost their footing when the water was only stirrup level, though some have crossed successfully when it was even higher.

I tried crossing the river when it was just over stirrup level once, and Cruiser stumbled and we both went under. I learned my lesson that day. The bad thing was that we came out on the far side, and the only way home was to re-cross the river. I was lucky to find a couple of other riders to follow back across the water. Even with their help, Cruiser was reluctant, but he didn't want to be left alone and so he finally plunged in. He cantered across and scared me to death, but we got to the other side safely. For several weeks he was hesitant to cross in that spot. I have never crossed it when it was that high since. Common sense must prevail, and some things are just not worth the risk.

A sensible person riding alone who encounters a river or flooded creek that she is hesitant to cross, because it is either too high or unfamiliar, should not make the attempt. If an accident were to happen, there would be no one to help. Of course, throughout the centuries, plenty of horses have had to ford deep rivers and raging creeks because there weren't any bridges. A horse can do it. However, if crossing isn't absolutely necessary, you owe it to your horse to keep him out of dangerous situations and to your family to keep yourself safe. We seldom have to depend on our horses for transportation; we ride them for pleasure. There are plenty of things we can do with our horses—why risk danger if we don't have to?

I watched in horror one day from the top of a hill that overlooks the river as three teenagers tried to get their mounts into the water. The river was higher than I ever imagined was possible. I stayed there so I could be of some help if an accident happened. The riders must have tried to beat their horses across for five minutes before they gave up. The horses planted their feet and absolutely refused to budge. It is possible that those horses saved the teens' lives that day. It is a good thing that at least the four-legged part of the group was concerned with safety!

CROSSING WATER SAFELY

If you have determined the river is at a reasonable depth for crossing, allow your horse to pick his way through the water. If you frequently cross in the same area, you may notice that he takes nearly the exact same route every time. I believe a horse memorizes the footing and feels safer—which he is—when he knows what to expect.

When there is a strong current or deep water, start crossing upstream of the spot that you want to arrive at on the other side. The current will prevent your horse from fording straight across. By traveling at an angle, you will end up closer to where you want to be. If you cannot enter the water upstream, try pointing your horse to a spot on land farther upstream than you actually want, and you probably will exit the river near where you originally intended.

If you are riding with friends, let the more experienced horses go across the water first, and the green horses will follow with much more confidence. The

Photo © Darlene Wohlart.

I allow Mingo to slowly pick his way across the water. Photo by Ellen Daly.

Travel across high water with strong currents at an angle so you won't get pushed downstream.

experienced horses may even know the safer routes to use, while a green horse is just learning. Let him learn from the pros.

There is nothing wrong with allowing a horse to drink; in fact, you should encourage it. But if he starts to paw, boot him forward immediately. Pawing is a prelude to rolling. Horses are most inclined to roll in water when they are itchy with sweat, so be extra cautious on hot days.

A horse should always quietly walk when going up and down river or creek banks. The footing can be hazardous, and you may not know what is at the top of the bank until you get there. Not only is it good discipline for your horse; it encourages better behavior from other horses in your group. One day, I was riding a green horse, and my sister Ellen was riding a veteran. Her horse caught her by surprise and decided to dash up a riverbank. My mare tried to follow at equal speed, but when she saw some mud, she panicked and made a tremendous leap to

> Never cross water while your horse is wearing a tie-down. He will need to get his head above water if he trips or steps into a deep hole. The tie-down, quite literally, can kill him.

get over it. I got a saddle horn in the abdomen. It served as a good reminder to be careful in these situations.

Even experienced horses that know they should walk will sometimes surprise their riders. I've found that merely sitting back, taking light contact on the reins and saying "walk" before starting up or down a bank will deter a well-behaved horse from going faster. If your horse does succeed in racing up or down a bank, turn him around and practice until he gets it right. It seldom takes long to teach this lesson, but you may have to repeat it again in the future.

RETRAINING THE RELUCTANT HORSE

I rode on trail for several years without realizing that crossing water could be a serious problem. Although the trails I used went alongside a river, it was quite some distance before they actually crossed it. Since my horse was fine with crossing and few people at my barn rode that far, I was completely oblivious to the fact that some horses are afraid of water. In that area of the park, the biggest obstacle was going under an extremely noisy highway bridge. If we could do that safely, we knew we had a good trail horse.

When I moved, I rode my new green-broke horse, Cruiser, to my new barn rather than trailer him. I was able to coax him across the water because he was accustomed to following me everywhere. I just assumed that all horses

Caution: Never allow your horse to paw in the water. Pawing can lead to rolling.

There can be serious consequences to not keeping your horse at a walk on a riverbank. Mike had ridden long enough to know better, yet he allowed his horse to trot down riverbanks. One day, his horse trotted down the bank and just kept trotting right into the water where he slid on the slippery bottom. They had a very bad fall in the water, and his horse was lame for several weeks.

Give your horse his head when stepping into the water. Photo © Carien Schippers.

Walk up and down riverbanks.

were like him, and with a little patience, they would happily cross water.

The new barn was the one mentioned earlier. The first river crossing was only five minutes down the trail, and there was no way around it. A rider whose horse wouldn't cross water couldn't ride very far. In addition, there were four other places that had to be crossed within five miles from the barn.

That first summer, I saw a fair number of people standing on the riverbank trying to get their horses to cross. Usually they were new to the area or they'd just bought their mounts. I would try to lure the horses across with my own, with varying success. Most often, I never saw those horses again. The owners either gave up or moved their animals to a new location that didn't have water obstacles. The problem was interesting, and I spent a lot of time reading and talking to people in order to find a good solution.

There are a few things you can do at home before you venture out on the trail that may help you when you have to cross running water. The first thing I would do is to walk your horse through puddles. Although puddles aren't the same as running water, if he won't step in a puddle, it is quite unlikely he'll step in a creek. The tricky thing with puddles is that your horse is smart enough to know he can go around it instead of through it. Start with a large puddle that is harder to walk around. You can cross it while in the saddle where you have better control of his body, but if he is trusting horse, you will be better off leading him on foot in the beginning. There is no way he will follow you through it unless you are ready to get your feet wet, first. Be patient and encouraging. Practice it until your horse doesn't seem to care whether he is in the water or not.

The next step is to create your own little creek by simply using a garden hose on the ground as your running water. A horse that is comfortable with a puddle may still be anxious about running water. Begin by running the water in a thin stream, and give your horse time to examine the water and satisfy his curiosity. While he is getting accustomed to the water, you can groom or massage him to make this a positive experience. When he looks relaxed, it is time to lead him over it. Go back and forth and gradually increase the size of the flow as he shows he is not worried. Finally, repeat the entire sequence while mounted. Be ready to back off at any point if your horse appears nervous.

This does not need to be completed in one day. Some horses work better when increasing the difficulty of task if they can think about it overnight. Other horses progress faster. By using your observation, you will know when your horse is ready to advance. To further challenge your horse before you try a real creek or river, you can also dig a trench or run the water over a tarp to make the obstacle more difficult.

If you are fortunate enough to have a stream nearby, there is very gradual approach that you can take. This is something that works well with a very young horse that you haven't started to ride yet, but you are looking for productive things to do. Take your horse down the water on a long lead rope, relax and let your horse graze. Don't try to get him in the water, just encourage him to be near it. Do this whenever you get a chance. Over a period of time, your horse will enjoy being near the water, and he may even step in it on his own. After a while, try leading your horse to the water and encourage him to drink or walk in it. When you are ready to ride or lead him across, he will be much more willing.

Without a doubt, the best advice I have found was from the well-known horse trainer John Lyons. His solution is simple and logical; I am surprised no one else mentions it. He suggests riding your horse as close as you can to the water, always pointing him to the exact spot you want to cross. Stop him when he shows signs of being fearful. Face the crossing spot, and let him stare at it for as long as it takes for him to become bored instead of scared. At that time, ask him to go closer. Keep repeating this until you get right to the water's edge. Allow him to sniff the water and stare at it until he is really bored. At that point, keep him there an additional five minutes for good measure. (Be sure to wear a watch because time will go very slowly for you.) Finally, ask him to go into the water and praise him profusely when he does. I did this with an older Quarter Horse mare, but I still couldn't get her to go in until I went first. I got wet, but it was worth it—she finally followed and got her sugar cube reward. The next time she went in with no hesitation.

Since I like stacking the deck in the trainer's favor as much as possible, I have added my own twist to the lesson in river crossing. Have a friend or two bring their horses to the river crossing about half an hour after you get there. This way, when your horse is ready, his friends will show him how to cross. This should work with most horses that haven't had a previous frightening experience. The joy to this method is that it avoids any form of confrontation and prevents your horse from forming any negative attitudes towards crossing water.

Your first water crossing with a new or problem horse should be well planned, not haphazard. Don't make the mistake of letting anyone talk you into doing something you don't feel your or your horse are ready for. It could have dire results. I have a very good friend who bought a high-strung, green-broke Arabian mare that was nine years old. The mare, Krystal, had no trail experience and little riding experience. One fine spring

After years of crossing the river by our barn, Cruiser unexpectedly slipped and fell. He scampered out of the water and waited for me to pick myself up and go to him. I got back on him and asked him to cross so we could continue our ride, and he told me he was too frightened to go into the water. Cruiser is the kind of horse that is always willing to go unless he is truly scared. When other riders came by and he wouldn't follow them across, I realized I had a serious problem. I didn't take him back to the barn; rather I rode him back and forth from the barn to the river a number of times at a brisk trot. (It had to be brisk because I was cold from my wetting.) As I rode I planned my course of action. I got home that evening and immediately called my sister. She promised to meet me out at the barn the next weekend, and we would try my plan.

I rode Cruiser down to the river by myself and we stopped at its edge. He refused to go any farther. I sat on him and simply waited. Just as planned, my sister showed up a half-hour later with Cruiser's best friend, Ranger. She rode Ranger across the river, and I asked Cruiser to follow. He was literally trembling from fear, but he stepped into the water and crossed over to the other side. It turned out that he was only afraid to cross the spot where he fell—nowhere else.

Stand and stare at the water as April is with Coco, until your horse is no longer afraid and very bored.

morning, a woman who boarded at our barn talked her into going on a trail. In a moment of weakness, Sharon agreed to go.

Things went well as they rode down the hill together. As they neared the water, the other rider told my friend she would take the reins of the Arabian and pony her across. Sharon, in another weak moment, agreed. The woman took the reins, marched to the river and tried to pull in the Arabian. As soon as the mare's feet touched the water, she went crazy, jerked backwards, broke loose, spun around and ran up the hill with Sharon hanging on for dear life with no reins at all! At the top of the hill, the mare ran across the street (thankfully there was no traffic) and into a neighbor's driveway. Then, realizing she was in the wrong place, the horse slammed on the brakes and spun so quickly when she turned for home that she threw her rider into the mailbox.

Thank goodness, the only injuries to my friend were a lot of bruises. The horse also was fine, but she became deathly afraid and nervous after incident, and it took all summer to coax her to cross the river.

Another friend of mine has a Morgan that had never crossed water before she bought him. Sometimes he would cross the river and sometimes he wouldn't. It didn't matter if another horse was with him or not. With the help of his stable mate, a horse wonderful with water, and the stable mate's owner, they decided to solve the problem. On a warm day, the two people, wearing shorts and old shoes, led their horses down to the river. They walked back and forth in it, playing and just having a good time for quite a while. At the end of the session, they were both assured that the Morgan was no longer afraid. The next day,

my friend took her horse down to the river. Once again, he refused to cross. She knew then he wasn't afraid—just stubborn. She firmly told him to go in, using a whip to reinforce her command. He never gave her a problem again.

Small creeks can be trickier to cross than large rivers because your horse may feel it is safer to jump over it completely to avoid stepping into the unknown. Be prepared for this to happen so that you won't become unseated. I have found that when a horse jumps anything that you don't want him to jump, the best thing is to go back and do it a few more times. Eventually, he will step into the water. Give him lots of praise when he gets it right and then go home.

Some people will circle their horse around and around until he will cross the water. At least, that is what they think will happen. I've watched people try it with their horses and never get a hoof in the water. I think the reason that it doesn't work efficiently is because you are punishing him by circling for being at a place that he is frightened. That only demonstrates to him that he was right and reinforces his uncooperation.

Some horses balk at rivers because they don't like to cross and have learned they can get away with refusing. They typically will go into the water fine if they are with another horse, so try to cross with other horses as much as possible and always praise your horse when he goes willingly. It is still important to have him eventually cross on his own. Usually he will try to turn as you approach the water. I've found it very helpful to put both hands way out to the side as if you are doing a leading rein with two hands. This makes it difficult for the horse to go in any direction except straight ahead. As soon as he hesitates, give him a firm kick, and

Here, as elsewhere, remember that you are teaching for the future. Your horse is not learning to cross water for this one time only, but for all the times to come as well. It is wise to give him the opportunity to face his fears. You may even decide to stop him in midstream after one or two crossings, so that he learns that he need not rush through water, it will not hurt him. Just don't let him roll!

he will probably go in. Once all his feet are in the water, stop him and give him a lot of praise.

Be prepared to use the same method if you are leaving a group of other horses to cross the water on your own. Even the most willing horse will be tempted to balk in such circumstances. We deal with this problem all the time, since not everyone in our neighborhood rides as far as we do. We'll ride with them up until the next river crossing, and then they will turn to go back home. Be prepared for the problem ahead of time. By steering your horse with two leading reins as explained above, you should be able to get him across. If worse comes to worst and you fail, don't go join the group and continue the ride with them. Stay at the water for a long enough time that your horse doesn't get rewarded by doing just what he wanted. Eventually, you can catch up with them, but don't let your horse make that connection. If you have a young horse, don't hesitate to get him into the water as soon as possible. The younger they are, the more open-minded they are. So don't put off that first water crossing because you don't want to get your feet wet. Give him the lesson as I laid it out for the riding horse. It's worth wet feet to have a cooperative horse when he grows up.

Use leading reins on both sides so that your horse can only go forward into the water.

CHAPTER SEVEN

Riding in Summer

Every winter, I dream about summertime. I imagine the warm weather and daylight that lasts until 9:00 in the evening so I can ride after work. By the time we are a couple of weeks into summer, the mild, warm weather I dreamt of is actually hot, humid and unbearable except in early morning and the late evening. Of course, those are the times when the bugs are the nastiest! So I start dreaming of fall. My employers beg me to use up my vacation in the summer when work is less busy, and don't understand why I want to wait until September and October when the weather is cool and the insects are few. To me that is paradise.

APPAREL

Riding in the summer in certain climates has its challenges, one of which is the comfort of the rider. Although we don't do the bulk of the work, we are still susceptible to the environment, and we must not forget to take care of ourselves. Heat exhaustion and dehydration affect people as well as horses.

The coolest clothes are loose-fitting cotton garments. If you want proper riding gear instead of regular clothes, check around for items specially promoted as cool summer apparel. Your tack shop may be able to help. Also check the mail order catalogs. Merchandisers are finding that riders need such items and are happy to supply us with anything that will make our lives more comfortable, at a price.

Wear sunscreen with a high SPF if you ride in the sun, and even on a shady trail if you are at a high altitude or you have particularly sensitive skin. Sunglasses are helpful, and a hat or helmet with a brim is indispensable. The lightweight, vented helmets are very cool and comfortable in hot weather. They are reasonably priced and well worth the investment in the interest of safety.

If the mornings are cool enough that you want to wear extra clothing, remember to layer for comfort, but don't remove any layers while on horseback unless your horse is already accustomed to this. To be safe, dismount before taking off your coat or sweatshirt.

Spend some time at home getting your horse used to you putting on and taking off clothing while mounted. You'll appreciate it when you're riding with others who do not want to stop while you dismount. Have someone hold your horse while you slowly take off a loose-fitting

A cool cotton shirt, a head covering with brim and dark glasses are essential rider gear for summer on the trail. Carry plenty of water and bug repellent, too. Photo © Linda Sherrill.

Depending on your climate, it may be prudent to always carry some sort of rain gear when you are out on the trail. Be sure to accustom your horse beforehand to the sight, sound and feel of your gear. You do not want him spooked by your flapping poncho.

jacket and put it back on. Talk to the horse quietly and praise him for calm behavior. Repeat this enough times that you are sure he is not frightened. At this point, begin training him to stand while you brush your jacket along both sides of his body, neck and hindquarters. Throw your jacket to the ground a few times to prepare your horse in case you accidentally drop a piece of clothing. (This will be easier if your horse has been sacked out during his early training.)

RIDING IN THE HEAT

During summer, I like to ride in the coolest part of the day and avoid the midday sun. Also avoid excessively hot days, or if you must ride on those days, ride slowly and watch for any signs of discomfort in either your horse or yourself. One summer, my horse was boarded in a stable where the ventilation was very poor. When I arrived on a hot evening, the horse would be sweaty simply from standing in his stall. We would go on a slow ride on the trail, and when we got back to the barn, my horse would be cooler and dryer than when we started. (I moved to a different barn shortly after that. It was one of the factors in my decision.) Slow and careful riding on hot days may actually benefit your horse in situations like these.

A study made before the 1996 Atlanta Olympic games showed that, when riding in heat and humidity, it is better to ride in the morning when the temperature is lower but the relative humidity is high versus the afternoon when the temperature is higher, but there is less humidity.

A good guide to the severity of the weather is simply to add the temperature to the humidity. If the sum ranges from

130–150 (54–66 Centigrade), you should be cautious. Be extremely careful if it is higher. When the sum is 180 or more (82 Centigrade), the weather is dangerous and you should avoid riding.

A horse's body (like a human's) cools by evaporating sweat. High humidity prevents evaporation—dripping sweat does not cool a horse. Humid weather makes heatstroke a potential hazard. Other causes of heatstroke include dehydration, overworking an unfit horse—particularly one with a heavy coat—or even simply standing in hot sun. Find a shady spot to rest your horse during hot weather and help him recover from exertion.

Horses, as well as people, adapt to the higher summer temperatures. As the weather starts to grow warmer, slow down and shorten your rides. Over time, you can gradually increase the distance and speed again as your horse adjusts to the heat and humidity. In early spring a horse will still have some winter coat left, and on a warm day he can easily become hot, even if you feel comfortable. Be careful not to overheat your horse on those warm days in late fall also.

A hot, itchy horse may want to roll while you are aboard; be alert and prepared. When a horse paws in the water, it usually means he wants to roll, so it is important to get him moving immediately. Once my horse tried it on dry land. She slowed down her walk and seemed interested in the ground, so I thought something was up, but I was still shocked when she went down on her knees. I stepped off quickly and smacked her, and she got up without rolling. She never tried it again, to my knowledge, but I have been particularly attentive since then.

It is wise, in hot weather, to keep your horse as wet as possible. I like to let my horses splash in the water when they cross rivers. You can increase the splashing by walking close to other riders' horses. In really hot weather, dismount and splash the horse's body with water by scooping it up with your hands.

Distance riders occasionally tie a scoop or sponge to their saddle with a long rope so they can dip it in water and wet the horse without dismounting. (If you decide to do this, get your horse used to the motion while you are on dry land. A river isn't the best place to spook your horse—you may find yourself cooled off more quickly than you wanted.) Since you're not in a race, why not take the time to dismount and splash? It gives your horse a chance to catch his breath, and you'll be cooled off, too.

DEHYDRATION

Dehydration is a problem for all trail riders. People in humid climates may be more aware of it because they can see the sweat dripping off their horse. Riders in dry climates may be deceived, though, because their horses don't seem to sweat as much. In reality, the sweat dries too fast for the rider to notice how much the horse is sweating. The sweating process isn't as efficient, and he continues to sweat profusely in an attempt to get cool. This leads to dehydration and can cause serious complications.

The surest way to assess your horse's state of hydration, is to perform what is known as the "pinch test." Keeping your horse's head and neck straight, pinch the skin on his shoulder area close to the heart and release it. It should pop back into position quickly, and within fifteen seconds the skin should lie completely

In hot weather, plan to ride where water is available every five miles or so. Photo © K. S. Swigart.

flat. You must first know your horse's normal skin reaction or the test isn't accurate. Any large variation from your horse's normal skin response is cause for concern. Know what is normal for your horse and do not wait for the first time you suspect dehydration to use the pinch test.

Other signs of dehydration are dry mucous membranes, dark urine and decreased gut sounds. More severe signs include sunken eyeballs, muscular weakness and slowed senses. The latter are very serious symptoms—your horse could go into shock. A mild case of dehydration can be treated by giving the horse small and frequent amounts of water. More severe cases should be treated by a vet.

To help prevent dehydration, allow your horse to drink as often as possible at river and creek crossings during the ride to ensure he stays hydrated. Ideally, a horse should be allowed to drink every five miles, but the environment doesn't always provide for this. In hot weather,

it becomes especially important to plan your ride so water will be available when needed. The river that I curse when it rises too high to cross or when it freezes in the winter is a welcome sight on hot days.

The old adage, "You can lead a horse to water, but you can't make him drink," is very true. However, you can tempt him to drink by stopping him in running water rather than in still water, getting him to relax a few minutes by slowing down the ride before getting to the water, and wading in very deep water. Riding with another horse that will happily suck up outdoor water may teach a neophyte trail horse that drinking water comes in other forms than in a bucket.

If your horse drinks his fill, keep him moving for the next fifteen minutes to prevent him from colicking. And always make sure your horse is cool at the end of a ride before you allow him to drink his fill.

If you are doing extensive riding in hot weather, you may want to ask your veterinarian about giving electrolytes to your horse. Electrolytes replace essential items lost in sweat and urination due to stress, heat and humidity. Because electrolytes can be harmful if used incorrectly, you shouldn't give them without your veterinarian's permission. He also can give you the best guidance for your particular horse, climate and the amount and type of riding you do.

Riders can become dehydrated, too. It is wise to take a big drink of water before you go out, and have some sort of liquid refreshment waiting for you at the barn or trailer. Water or a human electrolyte replacement such as Gatorade is best. Even if I only ride a few hours in the summertime, I spend the rest of the day drinking lots of liquids to make up for all the water lost by sweating. I want to make sure I'm fully hydrated. It is amazing how much water we loose through sweating when riding in summer. If you plan to ride for more than a couple hours, take some water along. You will find an assortment of insulated water bottles and canteens at your local tack store.

HEAT EXHAUSTION AND HEAT STROKE

Heat exhaustion is caused by hard work in hot and humid weather when your horse is unable to rid himself of the excess heat generated by his muscles. Poor condition and a heavy coat are contributing factors.

The symptoms of heat exhaustion include a high temperature, an anxious expression, shallow breathing, trembling muscles, blush-red nasal membranes and an unwillingness to move. A badly exhausted horse is apathetic, weak, unwilling to drink and exhibits signs of thumps. *Thumps* (also called *diaphragmatic flutter*) is a jerking of the belly or

The pinch test is done on the shoulder area. Pinch his skin and release.

flanks that is strong enough to be felt or even heard by the rider. It is an extremely severe warning of an advanced case of heat exhaustion and tells you to take action immediately.

You should stop your horse, cool him off by applying water to his body and giving him sips of water every couple of minutes. As your horse rehydrates, the thumps will disappear. The best way to treat heat exhaustion is to prevent it by riding smart as explained above.

Heat stroke starts with the symptoms of heat exhaustion. If the heat exhaustion is untreated, it will escalate into heat stroke. Your horse's temperature will skyrocket and, at the same time, he will lose his ability to sweat. If you are riding, he will pant and stagger. Dismount, find shade, remove equipment and begin cooling your horse. Splash water on his head and neck area and apply ice packs to his neck, flanks and extremities. Sponging his jugular vein (the grooves in the lower part of his neck) with cold water will help to cool his blood. Standing him in running water is helpful, too.

Medical help may not be available out on the trail, so it will be up to you to monitor your horse's condition to make sure it is safe to travel home. You should carry a thermometer in your first aid kit and a watch with a second hand. After your horse's condition has stabilized (temperature less than 102.5° F, heart between thirty to forty beats per minute, and respiration down to twelve or sixteen breaths per minute) you can start to lead him home. Check his vital signs every fifteen minutes, and if you notice them getting worse, stop and rest. If you are dealing with extreme weather conditions, it may be best to wait until the temperature cools off to start your trip home.

Without prompt and correct treatment, your horse can collapse and die. The importance of preventing heat exhaustion and heat stroke cannot be stressed enough, especially for the trail rider, since all too often veterinary assistance is far away.

Splashing in deep water is a great way to keep cool on a hot day. Photo © CLiX.

INSECTS

Insects are at their worst in the summer, so always use a bug repellant on your horse and yourself before a trail ride, and carry reinforcements along if the insects are really thick. Roll on or paste repellants are easy to pack in a saddle bag. Since every climate has its own tormenters, check with people who ride in the area and see what works best for them. Then experiment to see which product works best for your horse. Thin skinned and light colored horses seem to be bothered more by biting flies and mosquitoes than darker colored horses or those with normal skin.

Unfortunately, I have yet to find a really good repellent that keeps the serious bugs away. Many of the sprays seem to help repel the mosquitoes, but even though they do not bite, they still swarm around the horses and torment them. Deer flies rarely notice any repellent ten minutes after I spray it. Most repellents are formulated to protect against insects that haunt the stables, and they do that well, but it is different on the trail.

Fly masks are helpful for horses that become panicky about bugs flying around their heads. Some western bridles have small fly swishes attached. Some people use horse-tail hair crops to swish bugs away. I find these awkward to carry due to the different weight distribution compared to riding whips. Instead, I simply flick the bugs with my riding whip and swat them with my hands. If you would like to buy a swish, test one out at a tack store, rather than buying it from a mail order catalog, to make sure it will be comfortable for you to carry.

Of course, it should go without saying that your horse should have current vaccinations for West Nile, Eastern and Western Encephalitis, and any other immunizations for diseases native to the area and carried by flies or mosquitoes. Remember, mosquitoes are at their worst near water or wet areas and during early morning or late evening hours when the temperatures are most pleasant for riding.

I knew one older Quarter Horse that was so sensitive that his rider couldn't take him outside during the buggy months. Days that I didn't even bother to spray my horses, this horse would be frantically kicking at the few insects that were around. His rider tried everything to no avail.

If you hear your horse rapidly swishing his tail back and forth while you are riding, there is probably a horsefly that he can't reach on his back or the top of his hindquarters. Always check behind you when you hear those telltale switches. Your horse will be forever grateful if you kill the winged monster before it bites!

Holly is showing how a bug swisher works great for getting the insects off Patsy's face.

RAIN, THUNDERSTORMS AND LIGHTNING

Always be prepared for rainstorms, especially when trail riding in spring and fall. It wise to carry raingear with you at all times, and watch for sudden weather changes so you can take refuge if necessary.

Although it's best to avoid thunderstorms altogether, there will be times when you will be caught by surprise. No amount of listening to weather forecasts will protect you from all the storms. During volatile summer weather, keep an eye on the sky. Lightning is a very real danger. The fact is that you are much more likely to be struck by lightning than to win the lottery. Avoid lone trees and big open fields.

You may have to make a judgment as to whether to try to outrun an approaching storm, get off and lead your horse, or

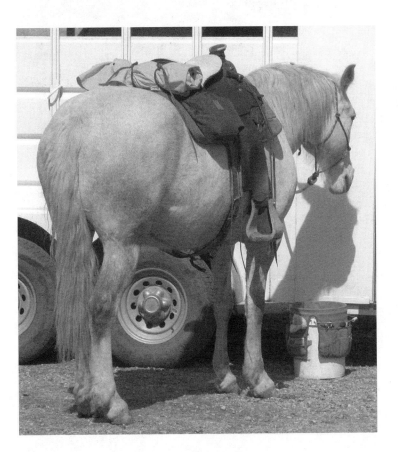

A rain slicker can be rolled and tied on the saddle
Photo © B. J. McKinney.

try to find a safe sheltered area and wait for the storm to pass. Don't try to outrun a storm if the terrain is treacherous. Find a sheltered spot and stay put, or dismount and carefully lead your horse to safer footing.

Even in the summer, and even in southern states, a sudden summer thundershower can cause a rider to become chilled. Hypothermia is a very real danger. This is why carrying rain gear to keep you dry, and an extra jacket or sweatshirt is so very important. Walking or jogging beside your horse will also help you to keep warm.

A person wearing a slicker can look pretty frightening to a horse that is not used to seeing it. Photo © Kim Andrews.

GRAZING ON THE TRAIL

Horses love to eat—who doesn't? However, they should not eat while you are riding on the trail. Not only does food interfere with the action of the bit, but a horse does not pay close attention to his rider and surroundings when he is

Dick was riding on a trail that ran right by the bank of a river when his Appaloosa mare reached over to grab a tree branch. As she swung her neck one way, her hindquarters swung the other way, and she stepped on the very edge of the bank. The weight of her body caused the bank to give way under her feet and she slipped down the bank to the river below. Dick tried to encourage her to climb back up the bank, but she couldn't. When he went down into the water with her, his feet sank into twelve inches of mud. That was what was keeping his horse from scrambling up. He had to lead her through the water, some of it up to his shoulders, for forty-five minutes until he found a way out of the river, and then he was stuck on the wrong side! It took him another half-hour of weaving through the woods before he was able to get over to the proper side of the water. All this because his horse decided to eat a branch!

thinking about when he will manage to get his next snack. I've been on horses that will try to grab a branch while at a canter or while negotiating a steep and rutted hill. They do not have their full attention on the job at hand, and the consequences can be serious.

Loose horses grazing in a field are very selective about what they eat, but a horse grabbing bushes and trees at random as he goes down the trail may bite into a toxic plant, something that has been sprayed with pesticides, or even a stinging insect.

To discourage this annoying habit, watch for your horse to reach for a bite to eat and stop him with the opposing rein. Pulling at both reins is not effective. A sharp word and even a tap on the neck with a riding crop may be necessary for serious offenders. Cruiser has learned not to eat if I am riding him, but if other people ride him he will take advantage of the new rider until they assert their authority.

It was extremely difficult to convince Mingo that he shouldn't be trying to eat as we ride along. We would be trotting along, and he would stop dead in his tracks to eat a tasty tree. Nothing I did helped. Finally, I couldn't take it anymore and turned to a more severe tactic. As he'd reach for a tree, I'd smack his lips with my whip. After a few times, the habit was broken (although every now and then he does need a reminder). He is now a much safer and more pleasant horse to ride. I do not recommend this technique except as a last resort, and then only if you are very accurate with your whip.

Another thing I often see is a horse grazing with a rider is on his back. This is not a safe habit. If the horse were to become startled and jump or run, the rider has no control because the reins are too long. Although letting your horse

A horse that grabs leaves could eat something toxic. Don't let your horse nibble on the trail. Photo by Ellen Daly.

With your reins this long, how quickly could you get your horse under control if he spooked?

A lightweight rope halter fits comfortably under most bridles. Photo © B. J. McKinney.

COOL DOWN SLOWLY

Always, always, always make sure your horse is cool when you finish your ride. If he isn't, lead him around until he is. A horse is cool when he is no longer sweating and his chest is cool to the touch. Putting a horse away when he is hot can cause colic or laminitis, two life threatening diseases. I typically walk the last fifteen to thirty minutes of a ride, depending on the temperature and how hot my horse is because I prefer to take longer getting home than to lead him around the stable. Walking also instills good habits in your horse by encouraging him to relax and not rush towards home.

After dismounting, offer your horse a pail of cool water. When he has dried, brush off the salt and sweat that accumulated under the saddle and girth. If it is really hot and you have time, your horse will love a cooling shower with a hose, or just having his back sponged with cool water from a bucket. Don't allow him to drink or eat his fill until he is completely cool.

graze may seem like a kind thing to do to, it isn't worth the risk. Instead, bring a halter and lead rope and let your horse graze while you dismount for lunch or a break. This will rest your body, too. A halter/bridle is perfect for this. You simply take off the bit and hook up the lead rope.

CHAPTER EIGHT

Riding in Cold Weather

Many people either don't ride as much in the winter or only ride in their safe and comfortable indoor arena. Some people quit riding entirely. Depending on your climate and how tough you are, you may be able to continue trail riding throughout the winter. Snow and cold do not necessarily spell doom for trail riders. Snow is beautiful to look at, and you will find the trails quiet and very peaceful. There are no insects and far fewer people around. Allergy sufferers will have a much more pleasant ride. It's also nice to see the old, familiar trails dressed in their winter "clothes."

RIDER APPAREL

The key word when dressing for winter riding is layers. Once proper winter dressing is learned, you may find yourself wanting to hike, skate and ski, too, because the weather no longer will seem so daunting. Dressing in layers turns you into a human thermos, keeping the cold air out and the warm air in. If your inside layer is one of the new moisture-wicking fabrics, even better.

When I first started winter trail riding, I found that the hardest things to keep warm were my hands and feet. I have a genetic condition called Raynaud's syndrome. It is a circulation problem; in cold weather, my hands and feet go numb in a matter of just a few minutes. As they thaw out with vigorous exercise such as riding, they are extremely painful. Until I solved this problem, I couldn't enjoy winter riding at all.

Winter riding is not for the vain horseman. Pack away those stylish English and Western riding boots you wear the rest of the year. Choose well-insulted boots roomy enough that you can wear at least two pairs of socks comfortably, but not so big that they won't fit in your stirrups. A completely waterproof boot is not always best choice unless your winter includes going through a lot of wet areas. The goal of waterproof boots is to keep your feet dry from outside elements, but they backfire by making your feet sweat, which in turn can make them incredibly cold. A water-resistant boot will work much better. Make sure your feet are warm and dry before you put on your boots. This will give your feet the best chance to stay warm once you are outside.

Wear two pairs of socks. The inner pair should be made of thin, sweat absorbing material, with heavier socks on the outside. Thinsulate ski socks are a

Warm gloves, layered clothing, a scarf, weather resistant boots and a warm head covering are essentials for winter riding. Photo © Joe Andrews.

great choice. Avoid cotton and acrylic socks because they become soggy and cold when your feet sweat. Wool socks work great since even if they get wet, they will still be warm, and they won't itch if you use them as the outside layer. English riders should have rubber stirrup inserts for their irons because plain metal will numb your feet. Western riders can invest in lined stirrup covers called tapaderos or hooded stirrups for extra warmth. You may want to change your stirrups to a larger overshoe type in winter so that your boots can more easily fit the stirrups. Never ride with stirrups that are so narrow so you feet will not slip out easily in an emergency.

If you find your feet getting numb as you ride, remove them from the stirrups and move them around to get the circulation going. If your feet get really cold, dismount and lead your horse for a few minutes. Don't make the mistake of riding with your feet out of the stirrups when they get numb and then jumping to the ground—it is surprisingly painful. If you take your feet out to move them around, put them back in the stirrups for a few minutes before

dismounting to prevent the painful landing.

If your horse goes well, you can ride in those fluffy poly gloves. Make sure they overlap the edges of your coat sleeves so no skin is exposed. Even people who ride English should train their horse to neck rein so they can wear suitable gloves for cold weather trail riding. With my sensitive hands, I find it essential to be able to neck rein with either hand while I put the other in my pocket, alternating hands as I ride. You can also layer your gloves, with a thin glove or a half glove underneath a weatherproof outer glove.

If your horse requires more precision riding, invest some money in special winter riding gloves that are available, and be sure to layer these as well. Many mail order catalogs sell special winter riding apparel. I spend a lot of time perusing these for way to make winter riding even more pleasant.

When you ride in the cold weather, always wear something on your head. Somewhere between fifty and eighty percent of body heat is lost through your head, so keeping it covered is crucial. I always ride with a helmet, but since it's one of those cool, vented helmets that works so well in the summer, it is of little use for warmth. One good choice is a hooded sweatshirt or polar fleece hooded jacket worn under your coat. Pull the hood over your head and then put on the helmet. Not only will this keep your head very warm, it keeps the sides of your face and neck warm, too. Recently, my sister bought me a helmet warmer. It's a combination of a hat, earmuffs and scarf all in one, and I just love it. It slips over my helmet and goes down to my neck, covering my ears, attaching with Velcro under my chin.

Thermal underwear is a must for winter riding. Wear it with loose pants that don't cut off circulation and that will allow a layer of warm air between your skin and the cold. Unless you wear high boots, it helps to put leg warmers over your pants.

Your torso is easy to keep warm. Just put on a thin layer, such as a T-shirt or thermal shirt, then a sweatshirt or lightweight jacket and finally a heavier coat. The jackets should have an adjustable neckline, such as one with a zipper, to vent out the overabundance of heat you will create if you do any vigorous riding. A scarf works well, too, for venting heat. Make sure you can move freely and comfortably while wearing your winter ensemble so that you can ride correctly and react properly. You don't want to be like the boy in the movie *A Christmas Story* who was dressed so heavily that he couldn't stand up after a fall.

Wise trail riders always carry an extra mitten or scarf, in case the ones they are wearing get wet or lost. Depending upon the climate, you may want to keep a rain slicker on the back of your saddle at all times. Cold winter rains, even in southern climates, are a major cause of hypothermia.

HORSE CARE AND EQUIPMENT

Not only should you take extra precautions when riding in cold weather; you must consider your horse as well.

Organized rides in late fall and early winter are often held in prairie grasslands such as this. Photo © Kim Andrews.

A cold bit is uncomfortable for your horse and may make him difficult to bridle. You can warm your bit with your hands and by blowing on it. Another option is to switch to a rubber bit, a bosal, or a mechanical hackamore. (Give your horse a chance to get used to any change in tack before you go on a trail ride.) I warm my bits with a hair dryer that I keep in the tack room.

Never work your horse too hard in extreme cold or deep snow unless he has been conditioned gradually and is in excellent physical condition. If you do work your horse hard in cold weather, make sure he is cool and dry before you finish. The long winter coat can make your horse quite hot and sweaty. Give him only a small sip of water while he is hot, then walk him until he is dry. Never put a blanket over a wet, sweaty horse and return him to his stall or turnout. If you have a lightweight blanket or cooler, put it over your sweaty horse while you walk him, and when he is nearly dry, remove it and brush him out. Then put on his stable blanket if you use one, or turn him in his stall or paddock.

When removing your saddle in cold weather, keep the blanket in place while you put up the saddle to give your horse's back a chance to adapt to the abrupt change in temperature.

Depending on the climate, the kind of riding you do, and how prone your horse is to sweat, you may want to consider body clipping your horse so he won't get as hot and will dry faster. When not working, a clipped horse must be blanketed. If you ride in extreme cold or snow, you can purchase a longer saddle blanket that extends over the horse's croup.

One of the drawbacks to snow is that it snowballs in the hooves of horses, especially those wearing shoes. The snow gets packed in round mounds of ice and your horse feels like he is walking on stilts. The phenomenon is at its worst on sunny days when the temperature is around the freezing mark; that is, the days that are so delightful for us are the worst for our horses. Greasing the bottom of your horse's hoofs with butter, shortening or non-stick cooking spray will help, but only temporarily. If this is typical weather for your climate and you feel you must have shoes on your horse, discuss other options with your farrier. Special shoes and pads available to help prevent snowballing, and your farrier will know what is best for your particular weather. Flat pads and those with convex bubbles decrease traction. Foot pads with a tube-type rim that conforms to the inner edge of the shoe keep out snowballs, allow the foot to function naturally and do not reduce traction.

Most people can get by with keeping their horse barefoot in the winter. It depends on the amount of riding you do, how fast you go, how much snow you get, and whether the ground freezes. Also, the nature of your horse's foot will dictate whether he needs shoes or not. Some horses can be ridden without shoes even in the summertime, and others need them all year long, even if they are ridden in a soft arena most of the time. If you have already pulled your horse's shoes for the winter and later want to ride in a rocky or slick area, Easy Boots are a good solution. You'll want to keep a pair of these around anyway, in case your horse throws a shoe on the trail or just before a ride.

If you ride often in icy conditions, ask your farrier about special shoes or studs that are available for horseshoes. However, these can cause injury if your horse stops quickly. The traction is actually *too* good. Even just turning your horse out to play when he is feeling frisky can result in injury if he is wearing studded shoes. Personally, I feel it is better to avoid ice and protect your horse's legs.

TERRAIN

Riding on frozen ground is like riding on cement, and you should be extra cautious that you not harm your horses by doing fast or excessive work. I prefer to walk when the ground is frozen and there is no snow to cushion my horse's feet. However, I get freezing cold due to poor circulation if all we do is walk. So, since I also enjoy hiking, I combine my two hobbies by tacking up my horse and taking him hiking with me. I ride him on hills and when crossing water, and he seems to enjoy walking beside me when we're on flat ground. This certainly impresses the dog walkers we see—most of their dogs do not walk alongside as obediently.

It is fine to trot and canter through deep snow. Even an inch of snow helps cushion your horse's footfall. If it snows before the ground freezes, this will delay freezing because snow acts as an insulator, and that makes trail riding possible further into late fall and winter.

Always be on the lookout for ice when you are trail riding in the winter. Try to stay out of low areas where water might collect. High ridges are good, since not only is ice less likely, but also the snow isn't as deep. It's wise to stay on familiar trails because snow can hide potential dangers.

Memorize your terrain and be alert. Remember that holes, ditches, logs and other obstacles may be disguised by snow cover. My horse once stepped in a

This unshod horse is wearing Easyboots on all four feet. Photo © B. J. McKinney.

Deep snow gives your horse an excellent workout even when he is not going fast. He must free his legs from the snow with every step he takes. Six inches of snow on even ground will work your horse as intensely as a climb up a steep hill.

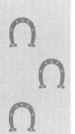

hole at the beginning of the trail. I knew about the hole since we had walked by it many times in good weather, but this time I wasn't paying attention. Thankfully, we were not injured because as soon as my experienced trail horse felt his foot sinking too deep, he stopped and lifted it out before it hit the bottom. I was lucky. Just a few weeks earlier, a stable mate stepped backwards off the trail into a ditch that was obscured by the snow. As his foot slid into the ditch, he went into reverse and backed right down into it. His rider then slid off his back.

Avoid icy areas, either solid ice or ice that may lie underneath partially thawed snow. Photo © Kim Andrews.

In some areas, plowed country roads are a good choice for trail riding in winter. There, you don't have to worry about hidden dangers under the snow, and traffic is often minimal. Photo © Joe Andrews.

This leads me to my next point: Know your horse. Some horses cannot be trusted when the going is treacherous; others cause you no worry at all. You will have to actively guide the former on winter trails. With the latter type of horse, of course you still need to pay attention, but you can thank your lucky stars for your good mount.

As snow thaws and then refreezes, a crust forms on top that I'm sure everyone living in a cold region has seen. This thick crust can actually cut a horse's legs and should be avoided. One winter we were snowed in for a few weeks and couldn't ride. The first break in the weather gave us good temperatures, but a very thick crust on the snow. I was so determined to ride that I went out in the field by the barn on foot and stomped out a path. It was a lot of work, and I was exhausted, but it was worth it. Until we got a real thaw, my sister and I just rode up and down that path.

HYPOTHERMIA

Even thinking about hypothermia makes me shiver. A sudden drop in body temperature can easily kill a person in two hours. This is not only a threat in extremely cold weather, when most people are careful to dress in layers and keep dry, but the real risk occurs in weather for which the rider is unprepared. The potential for hypothermia exists in weather as warm as fifty to sixty degrees Fahrenheit, and it is even more likely to occur during cool, rainy weather.

If you feel very cold, the best thing you can do to warm up is to stay as active as possible. Either ride fast or dismount and lead. To really get a good boost of heat, jog while leading or lead your horse up a steep hill. Try to stay dry and, most importantly, keep your head dry with a hat or helmet. Foods that are high in carbohydrates aid in

A ride that stands out prominently in my mind was, of all days, on the first day of summer. The forecasters predicted temperatures in the seventies, with a chance of rain. It was my birthday, and as a treat, I took the day off from work to go riding. The weather sounded perfect. I got up early and went out alone, wearing a sleeveless shirt and jeans. It was a cool morning, common for June in my area, and I expected it to warm up quickly. Instead, it never got higher than the mid-fifties. I wasn't uncomfortable, though, since riding kept me warm. The problems began an hour and a half from home when it began to rain. I wasn't carrying any rain gear, and in fifteen minutes, I was soaked and shivering even though we were moving at a brisk trot.

Luckily, I was aware of the risk of hypothermia, so to stay warm I rode as fast as was safe in the slippery conditions. When I became really cold, I got off my horse and led him, which helped me warm up again. When we finally got back to the barn, I made sure my horse was dry and comfortable and then rushed to my car and turned the heat on full blast. Unfortunately, I didn't have any dry clothes with me. Since then, I have learned to at least carry a spare jacket and sweatshirt when there is a chance of rain.

producing body heat, so if you're feeling cold, have a snack.

The symptoms of hypothermia begin with uncontrollable shivering and progress to disorientation, slurring of speech, skin cold to the touch, weak and irregular pulse, slow and shallow breathing and, ultimately, unconsciousness. Even if you have taken precautions and aren't in much risk of getting hypothermia, keep an eye on your companions. A rider can be shivering out of control and still not realize the threat. By keen observation and a quick response, you may be able to prevent a catastrophe. If leading the horse doesn't seem to help, or if your companion is in the more advanced stages of hypothermia, wrap her up with blankets or whatever you can find and gently rub them over her body to stimulate her circulation. If she is already unconscious, treat the victim for shock by raising her feet and lowering her head. Get medical help—this is a 911 situation.

Consider keeping dry clothes in your trailer or at the barn, as I now do, so you can change when your get back from your ride if you are soaked by rain or snow. Even if you are not heading down the road to hypothermia, it feels good to put on dry clothes.

Walking beside their horses is helping these riders warm up. Photo by Kevin Curry.

CHAPTER NINE

Handling Trail Emergencies

The vast majority of trail rides go without a single emergency. Even if a rider falls when a horse does something unpredictable, the worst result is usually a few cuts, bruises and shaky knees. A horse may trip, slip and even fall, but he will get back on his feet and continue as if nothing ever happened. Horseback riders seem to be blessed with their own guardian angel. Falling from five feet in the air, usually while in motion, should frequently mean a trip to the hospital. Somehow, it seldom happens. However, for those rare times when there is an emergency, it's best to be prepared.

Preparation should include some type of emergency first aid training, or at least carrying an emergency manual with you. Always let someone know where you plan to ride, how long you expect to be gone, and when you expect to be back home. Carry a map of the area and some emergency preparedness equipment such as matches, flares, water purifier or filter, a sharp knife or all-purpose tool, whistle, and a space blanket when riding in semi-wilderness or isolated areas. Always keep a halter and lead rope on your horse or in your saddlebag.

If an emergency occurs on the trail, the first thing to do is keep calm, and keep your horse as calm as possible. Don't panic. Panic causes people to make hurried decisions that are not thoroughly thought through and may not be in the long-term interest of horse or rider. Stabilize the situation and any injuries as best you can, then decide whether to call for help, and what kind. Should you: Call 911? Phone your veterinarian for advice? Call someone to bring a vehicle or trailer nearer to your location if possible? Walk to the trailhead?

Make sure that an injured rider is not in a life-threatening situation. If not, administer what first aid you can. Everyone in the group must work together. For example, if a horse or rider have fallen down a cliff and are not seriously injured, you may be able to use your lead ropes to pull them out. If a rider is injured but not the horse, ask the person most knowledgeable in first aid to attend to her injuries while someone else checks the horse over and ties it up safely. If a horse is injured, and you must call for veterinary assistance, stabilize injured limbs, apply pressure bandages to bleeding wounds, and stabilize the animal as much as you can in as safe an area as possible. It may take quite some time for the veterinarian to arrive.

77

By now, you probably see several good reasons to carry a cellular telephone. I would definitely recommend it for anyone who is riding in a place where help is not readily available. (Keep in mind, however, that in remote areas, you may be moving in and out of the phone's range.) Cell phones are not very expensive for the peace of mind they bring, and they can be lifesaving. Most newer models are very small and can be inserted in your saddlebag. It may be better to keep it attached to your body, though, in case you part with your horse. I do recommend that you turn off the ringer so as not to startle the horses, and tell your friends not to call you unless there is an emergency. Trail riding is a time to get away from things like telephones, pagers and all those hassles of life.

FIRST AID KIT

Whether you carry a first aid kit and what supplies you include depends upon how far you are riding and how accessible your ride is to outside help. Obviously, a trip out into the deep wilderness calls for more preparation than a ride in the city park or the neighbor's cornfield. If you are making plans for a long group ride, get together with your group beforehand and decide who should bring what. Between all of you, your group should be well prepared. Larger groups should appoint someone to be in charge of safety. Ideally, that person will be trained in emergency first aid.

Your first aid kit is limited to how much you can carry in your saddlebag. When choosing items, try to select things that will work for both humans and horses and that have a variety of uses. This saves both space and money. Something that is approved for human use is usually safe for a horse, but this isn't necessarily true the other way around.

These items take up a surprisingly small amount of room. You can carry your kit along in a traditional saddlebag, cantle bag, or anything that you can

These English saddlebags are large enough for a first aid kit plus snacks or lunch.

Trail Rider's First Aid Kit

- 4" x 4" sterile gauze pads
- Non-stick dressing pads
- Kotex (for bulk dressing) or cotton wrap
- Gauze-conforming bandages such as Vetwrap
- Betadine or Nolvasan and a large syringe
- Adhesive surgical tape
- Scissors to cut bandages
- Antibiotic ointment
- Cold pack
- Pantyhose
- Safety pins
- Sharp pocketknife or all-purpose tool
- Tweezers or small forceps
- Hoof pick
- Vaseline
- Thermometer
- Roll-on fly repellent (to keep insects out of wounds)
- Assorted sizes of band-aids
- Easyboot
- Package of water soluble electrolyte powder
- Aspirin/ibuprofen
- Desitin
- Wet wipes or towelettes
- Change to make a telephone call
- Snake bite kit if they are a threat in your area
- Bee sting kit or antihistamine if you are allergic
- Flashlight
- Waterproof matches or flares
- Ace bandage
- Eye wash drops
- Dental floss and stout needle
- Telephone number of your veterinarian
- Cell phone
- Personal identification and phone numbers
- Nutritional bar
- Cell phone if you have one

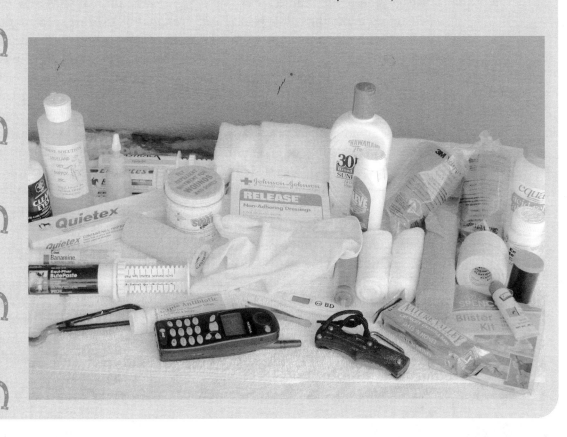

To keep things clean and dry, wrap the small items in Ziploc bags, then place everything in a larger bag tied with a twist tie, and place it in your saddlebag. If your horse falls in a river or if it rains hard, nothing will be ruined. Everything will be protected from dust and dirt. If quick action is needed, you can dump your saddlebag out on the ground to enable you to grab an item quickly without contaminating everything. One time, I had everything loose in my saddlebag. Someone needed to borrow a pen, and I opened up my saddlebag to get one. Before I could get it closed, Cruiser became startled by something and suddenly whirled around. Everything flew out on the ground!

carry on your saddle that won't bother your horse. There are some handy saddlebags for English saddles, even some that are sewn into the saddle pads. Treat yourself with something you really like and enjoy using. Don't provide any temptation to leave your first aid kit at home.

A handy, space-saving item is a pair of old pantyhose. They can be used to repair tack, as a sling, or as a cord, are lightweight and take very little room. Along the same lines, you might bring rawhide ties to repair tack, but end up finding other uses such as tying on a bandage or making a tourniquet. I know someone who used one to make a bit for her friend's horse. A creative person can do just about anything with a well chosen supply kit.

To save space, purchase small pill or liquid containers from a pharmacy and fill them with a small portion of medicine. Why bring a big bottle of aspirin, when a small bottle will work just as well and take up less room? You can save old prescription bottles or film canisters, rinse them out, and use them. Be sure to label them properly, not only as to the contents but also with how they are intended to be used. This way, if you forget, or someone else is using your first aid kit, there will be no confusion.

Betadine solution and hydrogen peroxide are old standbys used to clean wounds for both horses and humans. Bring along a syringe to aid in washing the wound. You can get one at any pharmacy. It is easy to use and you will end up wasting less solution than if you were pouring from the bottle. Neosporin or triple antibiotic ointment can be used on cuts and abrasions to prevent infection. Desitin will give relief for cuts, abrasions, rope burns, saddle sores and sunburn.

An item like an instant cold pack that is activated by squeezing is indispensable for many injuries. Cold packs should be used to keep swelling down. If you are going on a ride where you plan to camp overnight with your horse, it is a good idea to take several.

Easyboots can protect your horse's hoof if he loses a shoe. I suggest asking your farrier what size you should buy. Before you go out on your first trip with an Easyboot, try it on your horse's hoof to be sure it will fit. This will also familiarize you with how to put it on. It is best to learn at home, where your horse will stand patiently for you.

Periodically go through your kit to replace outdated items and anything you may have used. Always thoroughly check through it before a big ride. Keep anything that you don't think totally necessary at the barn or trailer where it is still somewhat accessible.

Always put some sort of identification in your first aid kit in case you are alone and unconscious, or your horse decides to go home without you. Even if you are riding with people who know you, they may not know your last name, where you live or a phone number to contact your relatives. Carrying a medical insurance card is another safety idea.

Tie a lead rope to your saddle so that in an emergency, you can secure your horse. Ride with or bring a halter or use a halter/bridle. Halter/bridles are handy, easy to use and relatively inexpensive.

ADMINISTERING FIRST AID

It is important to have a grasp of basic first aid principles. If you often ride in the wilderness, you should study a book on first aid or take a course to

---

CRASH COURSE IN EASYBOOT FITTING *Courtesy of EasyCare, Inc.*

Select a boot to fit your horse.

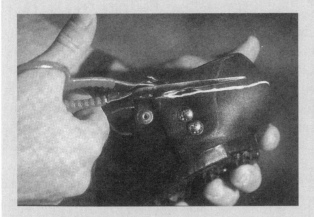

Cut down boot below hairline.

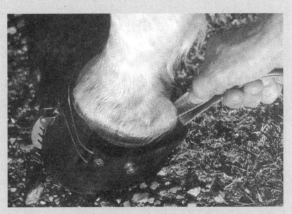

Use a one-inch piece of webbing to pull the inside strap around hard portion of heel below hairline.

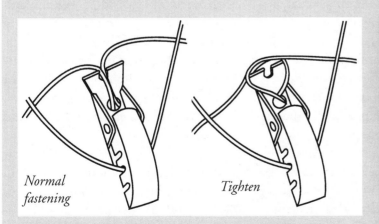

Normal fastening   *Tighten*

Snap buckle as tight as possible. You should not be able to open the buckle with your fingers.

Use a large flat screwdriver to remove Easyboot.

get more information than I am able to present here.

RIDER INJURIES

FRACTURES

A bad fall from a horse can result in a fracture. The signs of a fracture include severe pain, bruising, swelling or deformity. Don't take any chances. If you are unsure about whether there is a broken bone—if you think it might be a sprain or strain (damage to a muscle or ligament)—go ahead treat the injury as a fracture anyway.

The biggest danger sign with a fracture is if the area below the break becomes cool, pale or numb. This is an indication that circulation is impaired. This is a serious problem. The rider needs to be hospitalized immediately.

The first step in treating a fracture is to alter the clothing to let the injury swell. This may require tearing a sleeve or cutting the leg off the rider's jeans. Swelling is nature's way of making a splint. The only time this doesn't apply is an injury to the ankle or foot. In this case, keeping the boot on will act as a splint. If there is an open wound, cover it with a dry dressing.

If help can be obtained easily and quickly, make sure the injured rider is thinking clearly and is comfortable before going to get help. Leave someone behind with her if possible.

Otherwise, the injury should be splinted. A splint should start above the break and go below it. A couple of straight wooden sticks taped or tied together will work well. If such convenient items are not available, be creative. Anything straight and solid tied together with anything you can come across will work, such as a riding whip tied with bandanas or straight tree branches tied

with pantyhose. You can also use your belt or a stirrup leather from an English saddle. The injury can be padded by wrapping a saddle blanket around it.

If you suspect an injured or possibly broken arm, shoulder blade or collarbone, the arm should have a sling. You could pin the cuff of a long sleeved shirt to the opposite elbow. Creativity works well here.

If the injured rider can walk, let her walk to the barn or trailer. Under no circumstances should she try to ride. Not only will it be very painful; it can cause further damage.

BLEEDING

A fall that results with a nosebleed is easily remedied. Simply pinch the nose where the bone turns to cartilage for fifteen minutes and it will usually stop.

A rider who falls and vomits blood should be taken to the hospital at once.

Treating a bleeding wound is similar for both horse and rider. Apply a pressure bandage to the wound or wrap it with gauze bandaging.

An injury that is bleeding slowly with dark red blood is venous and should stop in ten minutes. Elevating the injured area will help.

If it is an arterial injury, identified by bright red blood spurting as the heart beats, hospitalization may be necessary. The loss of blood can be excessive and very dangerous.

Another danger sign is the same symptom as with a fracture: If the skin below the injury is cold and pale, it indicates a circulation problem and professional help is needed quickly.

If a rider's head is bleeding, don't let her lie down. Instead, keep her upright to help stop the bleeding.

Do not move any rider who loses consciousness from a fall. There may be a cervical spine injury and any movement of the head could cause permanent paralysis. The best thing you can do is to keep the person quiet and warm until an ambulance comes. Stabilize the injured rider's head with a hand on either side to keep it from moving it.

BEE STINGS

For most people, a bee sting is just an aggravation. However, an allergic reaction to a bee sting can be fatal. The swelling in the airways can cut off breathing. Rush the victim immediately to the hospital if any of these symptoms occur: dizziness, difficulty in breathing, flushed skin or hives. Anyone who knows they are allergic to stings should carry a bee sting kit with them.

Heat Exhaustion/Heat Stroke (see Riding in Summer, page 63)
Hypothermia (see Riding in Cold Weather, page 74)

HORSE INJURIES

WOUNDS

An open wound that is bleeding heavily should have direct pressure applied immediately with gauze or another absorbent material. Leave the dressing on the wound when it has stopped bleeding. If you remove it, you may cause bleeding to begin again.

A wound that is not bleeding should be cleaned with water or Betadine solution to remove any foreign objects. This is where a syringe is useful. Use the syringe to squirt the solution on the wound and wash it out. This is less painful than touching it, and you avoid embedding dirt in the wound. After the wound is clean, blot it dry with a clean gauze pad and apply some antibiotic ointment. If it is a leg wound or on any

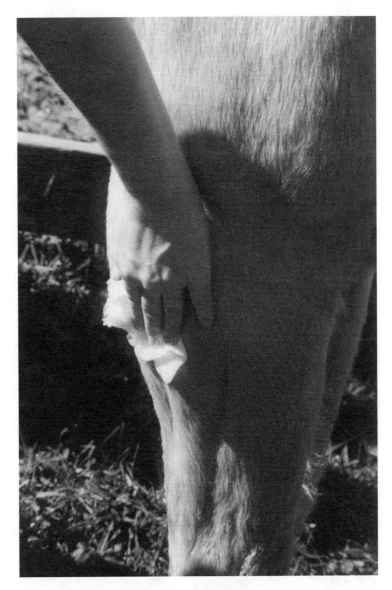

For a wound that is bleeding, use a piece of gauze to put direct pressure on it. Photo by Judi Daly.

other area that you can bandage, apply a non-stick dressing, cover with padding and gauze stretch bandage, and tape with a strip of elastic adhesive. Vetwrap is also an excellent choice for the top layer. Be sure not to pull the bandage so tight that it cuts off circulation.

FALLS

Having a horse fall with me has always been one of my biggest fears. Although it actually has happened to me three times without any serious injury to either my horse or myself, I am still terrified by the thought. I can replay all three incidents, second by second to this day. The first seemed to happen in slow motion. Although we were cantering, I still had time to think, "Oh no, this is my biggest fear. I'd better take my feet out of the stirrups and roll out of his way." I did just that and was on my feet to see Brandy stuck on his back like a turtle. I helped roll him over, and he was fine except for being sore for a week or so afterwards.

Be careful of falls when riding over steep rocky areas or on shale. Photo © K. S. Swigart.

If the unthinkable happens and it feels as though your horse is going to fall, the first thing to do is to kick your feet out of the stirrups. As your horse falls, push yourself away to one side and roll as you fall. Hopefully, you will be able to clear your horse, unharmed, and roll right onto your feet.

If you are caught underneath your horse, talk reassuringly to him to keep him quiet. The last thing you want is for him to panic with you in such a vulnerable position. Remove your loose foot from the stirrup and try to stay out of the horse's way as much as possible when he gets up.

An uninjured horse can jump to his feet as quickly as you can. As he rises, grab the reins so they don't interfere, and so he can't run away without you.

If your horse doesn't rise immediately, he is not necessarily dead or severely injured. His foreleg might be caught in a rein, preventing him from getting up. If his forelegs are tucked under his body, he won't be able to rise. Gently pull his legs out in front so he can get up. Perhaps your horse is lying still because he is frightened or the terrain is bad. Remove any branches or rocks that may impede him. Also remove the saddle and the reins, if possible, to make it easier for him to rise.

Before getting back on your horse after a fall, check to see if your tack is still in good condition and adjusted properly, and make any changes or repairs if necessary.

If you feel your mount start to slip or fall on a narrow trail, dismount quickly on the uphill side. If he falls or slides down a steep incline, try to reach him and keep him calm while you check him over for injuries. If he is down, see if you can get him to his feet and then check him over. If he can walk, look for a downhill route or a trail around the cliff. If there is no other way out, use your lead ropes and as many hands as are available to pull the horse back up the bank. If that fails, or if he can't walk, call 911. This requires a true emergency rescue.

Once your horse is on his feet, thoroughly check him for injuries and lead him for a few minutes to be sure he is okay. Look for any cuts or abrasions, and stop any bleeding with direct pressure on the wound, just like you would for a person. Clean the wound, apply ointment and wrap any leg wounds. Most other areas are impossible to bandage, but if it is summer, you may want to roll insect repellant in the area of the wound (but not in it) to keep the bugs away.

Run your hands down each leg to look for heat from bruising. A bad bruise may require an ice pack to keep the swelling down. I like to imagine what I would do if the same wound happened on my own body. A little nick on the leg doesn't require wrapping and a slight bruise is no big deal. My sister's horse, Ranger, fell once and skinned a large area of his shoulder. It was ugly at the first glance, but on closer examination, we realized the fall only took off the hair and one layer of skin. It didn't bleed. Since we were only half an hour from the barn, we waited until we got home where the would could be easily hosed off to doctor it. Our reasoning was that if the same injury happened to us, it would hurt quite a bit, but we wouldn't consider it an emergency.

LAMENESS

Another typical injury your horse may get is a sprain. A sprain is caused by overstretching or possibly tearing a muscle or ligament. If it is mild, it will cause him to limp slightly. In that case, apply a supportive leg bandage and care-fully walk the horse back to the barn or trailer and let him rest for a few days. A more severe sprain which causes your horse to have major difficulty walking means you should apply ice and get help. Hopefully, you will be able to get a trailer close to your location and haul him home.

When ridden in rocky areas, horses can get stone bruises on the sole of their hooves. An Easyboot may help get your horse home comfortably.

A LOOSE HORSE

A much more common occurrence than a horse falling is a rider falling, resulting in a loose horse. Never chase a loose horse on horseback, because it will give him reason to run. Instead, give your horse to someone else to hold and walk quietly to the loose horse, staying between him and your horse.

A woman once told me she always carries peppermints in her fanny pack, and she has trained all the horses she's ever ridden to come to the sound of the wrapper. I'm sure it takes all of five minutes for a horse to learn that a rustling wrapper means he will get a treat. If her horse gets away from her, she may be able to lure him back with the candy. Recently, her horse spooked and knocked her off. He dashed about one hundred feet away. Fortunately for her, he ran the wrong way, and she was between him and the barn. She pulled out her trusty piece of candy and started to open up the wrapper. His head went up, and he walked right to her. I think I'm going to get a bag of peppermints, myself. My horses already know what the sound means!

Try bribing him with grass, and talk to him calmly.

Usually a horse doesn't want to leave his stable mates and will not be in any hurry to get away unless he's really scared. If he runs, stay put to see if he will circle and come back to the other horse(s). If not, follow him slowly. Most likely he will eventually come back to the "herd." If you are riding alone and your horse gets away, don't blindly follow until you are both lost. If your efforts to entice him immediately fail, it is better to go for help.

One day I was riding a borrowed filly that, for no apparent reason, suddenly got out of control. She turned around and ran straight for my sister's mount, swerved sharply at the last minute and threw me into the other horse. The filly was running away and we were five miles from home. We didn't chase her, but followed on foot as fast as we could. A few minutes later (although it seemed like an eternity) she came back to us running even faster than she had left. She was afraid and needed her stable mate for security. I breathed a very big sigh of relief, and we continued home.

CHAPTER TEN

Conditioning the Pleasure Horse

This book is not about long distance riding, so you will not find advice here on conditioning your horse for a 100-mile ride. Instead, you will see what the average person needs to know to get their horse ready for an average trail ride, as well as some techniques used by distance riders that you can incorporate into your program.

EARLY RIDES

Before beginning any new regimen, you must assess your horse's current condition. He may be in fairly good shape from ring work. If you are riding three to four times a week for an hour each session and at least half of it is trotting, you are in a very good position to start trail riding. On the other hand, if your horse has been off all winter or is very young and you have just started riding him, you will have to start from the beginning.

Some people board their horses at stables with an indoor arena during the winter in order to keep them in shape for trail riding in the spring. I did that myself at times, but some winters my horses boarded at a place without an arena. I tried to do as much riding as I could in the inclement weather just to keep them

in some semblance of condition. Longeing a few times a week helped. Each spring, I would have to build them up slowly before we could go on any strenuous rides. This helped me build up my muscles gradually, too. The soreness we riders feel after the first ride following a few months off should remind us of how sore our horses can become if we don't give them time to build up their strength.

Begin with a lot of slow work, mostly walking, with some trotting and a small amount of cantering to break up the monotony. Be careful not to overdo it. It simply isn't worth the risk of injury to go galloping up a steep hill when your horse isn't ready. Even if the result for him (and for you, too, if you haven't done much riding recently) is only general muscle soreness, you may well harm his attitude towards trail riding. A trail horse with a good attitude is a joy to ride, and care should always be taken to maintain that attitude. You want your horse to enjoy it as much as you do.

While you are doing something as fun as horseback riding, time flies, and it is easy to go too far. A watch will help prevent that three-minute canter from turning into a ten-minute canter and that one-hour ride from becoming two hours. Just carrying a watch isn't good enough, of course; be sure to look at it before you start so you will know when you've gone far enough. Discipline yourself to turn around at that point. Keep track of the times so you can accurately increase your horse's workout instead of simply guessing.

It's handy to have a pad of paper at the barn or in your saddlebag to write down a description of your ride and how long it was. You can then easily refer to your records to see how your horse is progressing and determine what should be done on each ride without depending on memory. Simple entries like "Rode for one hour, trotted twenty minutes in five-minute intervals, was still frisky at the end," will give you a good overview. If you keep track of his TPR (temperature, pulse and respiration), you can write it here, too. It will be helpful in the future if you have to bring that horse up to condition again. You can also write down the various things in it that you are doing in the arena, so you can see how each horse is learning there as well. Memory can be faulty.

Walk through deep mud instead of trotting. Photo by Kevin Curry.

On the early rides where you intend to do a lot of walking, it is particularly helpful to bring a companion. The time goes faster with someone to talk to, and you will be less tempted to overwork. If you ride by yourself, you may get bored and want to pick up the pace when you shouldn't. Horses also are less likely to get bored and act up if they are with a friend.

Be very cautious of deep footing in the early days of conditioning. Some places will be unavoidable; these should be taken at a slow, careful walk. Charging through them can strain muscles and even bow a tendon. Green horses may panic when they sink in deep mud. Be prepared, and try your best to keep your horse quiet.

Many people don't have extensive trails at their stables and must trailer their horses to get to good ones. If this is your situation, unless it is feasible to haul your horse three to four times a week to trail ride, much of your conditioning will be done at home. The biggest drawback to this is, simply, that most horses get bored after an hour of ring work, if not sooner. In this case, I suggest riding no more than an hour in the ring but riding as many times a week as you can. Do your best to entertain your horse by working on a lot of figures and gait changes. Trotting over cavalletti and zigzagging around cones will add even more interest. Even a little jumping will add variety. All of these help to build muscle, too

Riding with a friend makes it more fun for both humans and horses. There was a time when my sister and I only had a round pen to ride in when we couldn't get down to a trail. We livened things up by both riding at the same time, one on the outside of the circle and the other on the inside going in the opposite direction. We were all challenged: My sister and I

*Ride with a friend.
Photo © Lourie
Ann Zipf.*

had the challenge of keeping our horses listening, and our horses had the fun of trying to thwart us.

If your stable has several riding areas, try to vary which one you use. It will also add interest to use several places during the same ride, for example, starting in the indoor arena and cooling off in the outside corral. If you do have a small amount of trail to ride on, take advantage of it by working a full hour in the arena and using the trail to cool down or warm up. Even doing the same trail a number of times can work. Horses don't seem to get as bored of trotting back and forth on a trail the way they do in an arena.

The river is only five minutes down the trail that I ride, so when high water or ice inhibits me, I spend a lot of time working up and down the hill leading to the river. I'm usually joined by other people doing the same thing. We all "work the hill" together and, as a bonus, we have a great time visiting. Most of these people, like me, have an indoor arena at their stables to use instead of the hill, but getting the horses outside onto the trail breaks up the boredom of ring work and helps with conditioning. Not only does using the trail extend your ride, but it encourages your horse to have a positive association with trail riding. He will see it as the fun part of a riding session when compared with routine ring work.

Another alternative to the arena is to ride on the road. The friends who adopted the retired police horses take them out on the streets of their neighborhood. The horses don't mind, since this was their venue for years when they were on the force. If your horse is good with traffic and your roads safe to ride on, you can use the road to warm up or cool down your horse and extend your ride. If it is necessary to stay on pavement, remember not to go any faster than a walk.

Riding along the road can help to condition a horse for trail riding, but always walk on pavement. Photo by Kevin Curry.

Pavement is slippery and causes considerable concussion on a horse's joints. Also, be respectful of people's yards.

LATER RIDES

Gradually increase the length of your ride by going farther and using faster gaits. Don't do too much cantering in the first month—it takes a lot of energy and will tire your horse far more quickly than a trot. In addition, particularly in the spring, horses get very excited and worked up when cantering. They are less likely misbehave or get injured if you keep them calm. Walking, trotting and hill work are the best ways to build muscles.

Try to go up as many hills as you can find, but don't let your horse gallop up them and risk muscle strains. Walking up hills is much safer and is still very effective in strengthening muscles. Gradually introduce trotting and cantering uphill. Keep in mind, however, that at any one moment in each stride of the canter, a single foot is carrying the all the weight of your horse. Imagine what would happen if the footing under him gave way at that moment. Have that picture in your mind when you are deciding which hills to canter up.

As your horse's condition improves, you can trot down some slopes as long as they are not very steep. Avoid doing this the first few months because it puts a lot of strain on his joints. Since a horse is not very balanced at the beginning of training, he is more likely to stumble. Do not allow him to rush down the hill; instead, take light contact on the reins and sit back to slow him down.

For the most part, just be sensible; build gradually and err on the side of caution. Be sure to walk the first ten to fifteen minutes of every ride to warm up and spend at least as much time to cool down at the end of the ride—more if your horse is really hot. Walking the last mile home also keeps your horse quiet. There is nothing a horse loves to do better than race towards home when the barn is close by.

A good rider is aware of the physical state her horse by monitoring, even if subconsciously, his every movement and attitude. Is he feeling full of himself, alert, relaxed, willing, sluggish, fatigued, crabby or irritable? My sister tells me when her horse is in a bad mood so I can avoid his heels, although from my position I can hardly see a change in his attitude, it is so subtle.

A horse's mood reflects how tired he is and will give you an idea when to rest and when you can pick the speed up again. My normally cheerful horse, Cruiser, may get crabby when he is tired or sore. As soon as he seems crabby, I let him walk for five or ten minutes until I feel a lifting in his mood. At that time we will trot, and he will move in his usual happy manner.

VITAL SIGNS

There is a specific, measurable way to see if your horse is coping well with his training program, and that is the TPR (temperature, pulse, and respiration) method of monitoring used by long distance riders. It can be helpful for any rider.

Temperature is taken with a rectal thermometer. Monitoring a horse's temperature is particularly important in very hot and humid weather. At rest, a horse has an average temperature of 100–100.5 degrees Fahrenheit (38 degrees Centigrade). This will go up with exercise, but if it goes over 103 degrees Fahrenheit (40 degrees Centigrade), the horse should be cooled down immediately by hosing him with water (or sponging him if this happens on the trail). Be familiar with your horse's normal at-rest temperature so you know what is typical for him.

The pulse is most easily measured with a stethoscope held just in front of the right side of the girth area, three to four inches above the base of the chest. If you don't have a stethoscope, you can check the pulse with your fingers by placing them over an artery where it crosses a bone. The underside of the jaw or the lower inside or outside of the foreleg is commonly used.

The normal, at-rest pulse for a horse is 36 to 48 beats a minute. Here, also, you should know your own horse's normal pulse. Take it at home when your horse is relaxed to give you a good starting point. The simplest way to do this is to count the beats for fifteen seconds and

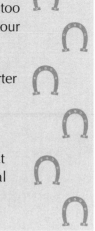

Signs that you have pushed your horse too hard and should let up on the intensity of your ride until he recovers include:

- Loss of coordination exhibited by shorter strides, stumbling, a sour attitude and muscle tremors.
- Palpation reveals sore muscles.
- Thick, sticky and musty-smelling sweat (a normal horse's sweat, after the initial sweat, is clear and even).

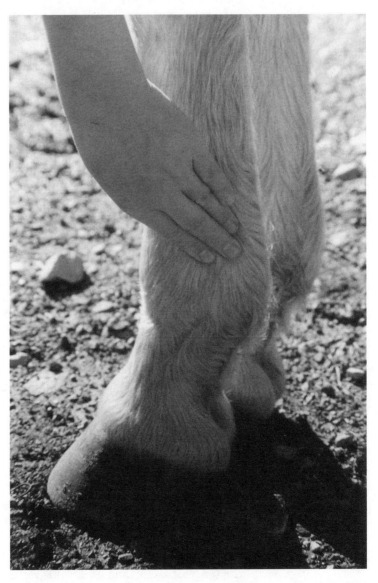

The inside or outside of the foreleg can be used to find the pulse.

multiply the result by four to arrive at beats per minute. Obviously, a watch that counts seconds is essential.

The heart is a muscle and in order to make it stronger, it should be worked to approximately 200 beats per minute for a short period. The recovery rate also should be monitored. After about a minute of rest, the pulse should fall to 120 beats per minute. If it doesn't, you have probably pushed your horse too hard. After a ten-minute rest, the pulse should be down to 72 beats per minute.

The third and final element in the TPR method—respiration—is much easier to measure because you can count the breaths by watching your horse's flanks, and you don't even have to get out of your saddle. One breath equals one inhalation and one exhalation. As with everything else, it is best to know what is normal for your horse. At rest, the average horse breathes 8 to 14 times per minute. Exercise will increase the respiration to possibly as high as 120 breaths a minute. The important thing is that within ten minutes of rest, it should drop to around 40 breaths per minute. After about an hour of rest, it should be close to normal. Never push your horse to the point where his respiration is higher than his pulse, for that is far too much exertion.

Monitor also the quality of his breathing. A horse takes deep breaths to get more oxygen. Shallow breathing indicates that he is trying to cool his body (much like a dog panting with his tongue out) and is the sign of an unfit horse. He doesn't get as much oxygen this way, and lactic acid builds up in his muscles, making him very fatigued. Shallow breathing is a telltale sign; it indicates you need to slow down for a while. Slowing down will aid in ridding the body of lactic acid and your horse will then recover.

With careful work, the rate of recovery should gradually improve. The better the recovery rate, the more fit the horse.

In addition to temperature, pulse and respiration, it is wise to monitor your horse's sweat. A fit, healthy horse has clear, fluid sweat on the neck, chest, flanks, under the forelimbs and the saddle area. Sweat that is frothy, sticky, gummy or patchy is a sign of a horse that is not in top condition. If your horse is not sweating in a situation where he should be, it is the sign of anhidrosis. Contact a vet immediately—this may be a life-threatening emergency. The condition can develop in as short a time as five minutes, so it pays to be observant.

DISTANCE RIDING TIPS

When on the trail, you should make a concentrated effort to switch leads. Because the canter uses a whole different muscle pattern for each lead, switching gives the muscles of the previous lead a rest when you ride the new lead. Cruiser will switch leads on his own with a flying lead change if we are cantering for more than a quarter of a mile. He typically gets an extra burst of speed that way. From a horsemanship standpoint, your horse should pick up either lead on request. If he doesn't, it is a good project to work on while you are on the trail. Use sharp bends in the same way you would use a corner of a fence for your canter transitions.

While posting, switch diagonals often. If you do a lot of trotting, even if you ride Western, learn to post because it is easier on your horse. Posting gives a break to the muscles on the side you are rising on. As a good rider, you should be able to post either diagonal. Miles of trail offer great practice opportunities, so take advantage of them.

Once you can post both diagonals comfortably, try variations such as rising for two beats and sitting one, rising for two beats, and so on. It may seem difficult at first, but you can do it if your seat is balanced. Anyone who finds it impossible should examine his or her riding. Ask a knowledgeable person to observe your basic alignment from the ground or have someone take a video—you may be surprised at what you see.

Posting without stirrups is another challenge. This is hard, but certainly possible. For years I believed that people who could do this were freaks of nature; I knew I would never be able to do it. Then I discovered my legs were poorly positioned. Once I corrected that I was able to post without stirrups, although it was still difficult. Riding position is not simply a matter of looks—the more in balance your body is with the horse, the less fatiguing it is for your mount and the less likely that you will cause him muscle soreness on long rides.

If your horse begins to show some signs of fatigue, he may only need a micropause, a short rest. Walking for a few minutes will help eliminate fatigue. It is surprising how lively a horse can become when you request him to trot again after a very short rest. I use this technique often when trotting or cantering seems to be the only good escape from insects. I trot a few minutes, walk until the bugs are unbearable, and then trot for a few more minutes. My horse thus doesn't become exhausted when going a long distance in a bug-infested area.

Don't trot your horse down slopes until he is in good shape. Larry's horse, Fire, is in a bit of a hurry to get home.

WEIGHT

As your horse's condition improves, you will see changes in his appearance. His coat will be sleek and shiny and his muscles firm with good definition. At the correct weight, there should be just enough fat that you can feel his ribs but barely see them. The point of his hip should not be visible.

Excessive weight causes your horse to work much harder. Fat traps heat by growing between the skin and the cooling mechanisms of the veins. Fat horses have a sweat that tends to be gummy and doesn't dry as fast, thus inhibiting cooling. These horses are at risk of overheating and take much longer to cool off at the end of a ride. If your riding time is limited, the length and quality of your rides could be reduced.

By doing a lot of trotting, Sharon is getting Beauty in condition without getting her overly excited.

It is better for a horse to be a little thin rather than too fat. If you are unsure about the state of your horse's weight, ask your vet. Many people feel they are being kind by feeding their horses excessive amounts of food, but they are really doing them a disservice. In many cases, a reduction of diet is really the kinder path to take.

Conditioning a horse involves not only exercise, but also regular health maintenance, including quality food, vaccinations, foot care, dental care and regular worming. Neglect any of these and a horse's ability to reach his potential is reduced. I also firmly believe that care and personal attention from the rider is essential for the horse to keep the right attitude. Mental health often goes side by side with physical health. So don't just ride your horse, spend some quality time grooming, training and just keeping him company. You'll be rewarded by many happy trail rides.

Section II

Training the Trail Horse

Photo © Kim Andrews.

CHAPTER ELEVEN

Starting the Young Trail Horse

Young horses are quite open-minded, and the early years are the most important years in which to introduce obstacles and challenges related to trail riding. The most difficult horses on the trail are horses that were ridden in a safe arena until their owners later decided to enter the outside world. Sometimes, by then the horses are well into their adult years, and they naturally become frightened and resistant on the trail. Serious problem behaviors can develop, and they can be dangerous to both horse and rider. If you have a foal or yearling that you plan to eventually ride on trails, take advantage of the time before he is ridden to prepare him. Everything you teach him regarding the trail at a young age will help in any other career you choose for him as well. An added benefit of taking a young horse on trail is that it's a great form of exercise for the human handler.

When training horses, I take my time and do new things in small, bite-sized increments. For example, I start trail horses by leading them on the trail, and move slowly from there. I build on each experience, so new experiences are rarely traumatic. In the end, I have a well-trained and confident horse. The time is well spent.

One day as my farrier, Ken, made a remark that really sums up my attitude about horse training. My sister's horse, Ranger, was very difficult to shoe the first few times. Ken was shoeing him and, for no apparent reason, Ranger was being a perfect angel. Ken didn't question his good fortune; he just worked as fast as possible to get the job done before Ranger changed his mind. It was a hot summer day, and he was exhausted and dripping with sweat. When he finished, my sister put Ranger in his stall while the farrier caught his breath. I jokingly said that if there was a contest for who could shoe a horse the fastest, he should enter it.

Ken replied, "They do have contests. The entrants will often trim and shoe four hooves in just a few minutes."

"That must be something to see," I said. "How do they judge it—on time alone, or do they take into account the quality of the job, too?"

"Just on the time," he answered. "It doesn't matter how well or badly they do, as long as they get all four shoes on. The horse could take one step and the shoes fall off, but the time still counts. In fact, after they're done, someone has to remove the shoes and redo them the right way."

It didn't occur to me at the time, but he was telling me something that applied to much more than shoeing horses. In order to be done correctly, most training must be done slowly and precisely. The majority of problem horses are created by trainers looking for a shortcut or those who are not patient enough to let the individual horse learn at his own rate. Usually the only solution is to go back to the beginning and do it all over again the right way.

In fact, this is true not only with horses, but with most things in life. Life has sped up so much in the last few decades that we expect everything instantly. In some cases it doesn't do much harm, such as fast food (although some reports indicate our health is suffering due to these meals) and paying at the pump with your credit card, but perhaps in the midst of all this rushing around, we are missing something. If we slow down a little, not only will we do a better job with less stress, we might learn to enjoy the journey just as much as reaching the goal. This is exactly how I feel about training horses—end of sermon.

Remember that your youngster doesn't automatically know what's acceptable in the human world—even in his own horse world, he has to be taught proper manners. This takes time. Patience, patience and more patience will help him learn what it is you expect from him.

LEADING

It is no secret that young horses have a very short attention span and can become easily bored and distracted. In that state, they usually become playfully resistant. By interspersing trail training into their basic training routine for variety, many problems caused by boredom can be prevented while simultaneously creating a great trail horse.

According to *The Horse's Mind* by Lucy Rees, a book that delves deeply into horse psychology and is a must for any horse owner, exploration is a key element in a young horse's life in the wild. Youngsters are very inquisitive and enjoy going on excursions. Rees feels that if we encourage this natural inclination we will teach our horses to be bolder and less fearful and anxious in their adult years. According to her, the second and third years are the most critical in this regard, and horses deprived of exploration during this time will tend to be afraid in new situations. It is so important to her that she recommends real schooling begin in the horse's fourth year, and all the riding time before that should be spent on the trail. This may be extreme for some people's training programs, but it makes a point: there is good reason to encourage the tendency to explore.

If your foal's dam is a quiet trail horse, some training may be done even before weaning. With help from a friend, you can lead the mother and baby for short walks as soon as the foal is halter-broken. Gradually introduce him to traffic and vehicles around home, and even accustom him to the sound of honking horns or racing engines. If possible, take both mare and foal to shows or other events so he can become familiar with that kind of activity. Avoid anything that may make the mother anxious, however, since your intention is for her to demonstrate to her baby that there is nothing to fear. Also, beware of getting the foal too excited or tired. It is important to give him much verbal praise and to reassure him with your touch. The goal is for him to equate adventures outside the stable with pleasure and prevent nervousness from the beginning.

After he is weaned, take your foal for short walks; start with easy ones and gradually increase the difficulty of obstacles and scary objects. The accompanyment of another quiet horse may be helpful for the first few walks to give your foal confidence, but eventually he should go alone with you. You want to shape a horse that trusts you and is independent of other horses. Many obstacles can be conquered early on instead of waiting until they become much more challenging as your horse grows older. Mingo, my Paint colt, was five months old when he went on his first trip to the river. We met a couple of trail horses from a different stable, and he didn't hesitate a moment in following them into the water. He wasn't afraid of water from that day on until the first time I rode him across the river and he fell in, but that's a different story.

Take the time to give your youngster an opportunity to examine the challenging obstacles that you encounter; don't rush him. He may become startled by all sorts of things, but fear will quickly be replaced by curiosity. That's the joy of working with a young horse. Turn him toward the obstacle and let him think about it for a few minutes. Soon he will want to approach. As he gets closer, praise him. He may want you to go first and he will then follow. This is good because your objective is to build his confidence in you as well as in himself.

Before you take your young horse into rugged country where he might brush against branches and bushes, accustom him to a whip lightly touching him all over his body. This should help prevent him from being startled when

This young horse is being ponied over a "bridge." Photo © Kim Andrews.

something accidentally brushes against him. You can even set up a brush obstacle in a safe spot at home to introduce him to the sensation. This has paid off with my horses. Now, if they get mixed up in branches or grape vines, they will calmly stand still while I dismount and untangle them. One day, I was riding Cruiser at a nice canter when I heard a funny noise. Whatever it was, it wasn't bothering him in the least. I was curious, and glanced behind us. He had tangled his tail in a small tree branch and was dragging it behind at a canter, yet he was completely unworried. It made me smile to know my work had paid off.

Be prepared for spooking—it's normal. When a young horse spooks, he will typically do one of two things: He'll

Watch for signs of fear in your youngster. You can often head off an explosion before it takes place. Tune in to your horse's warning signs: a short stride, refusal to go forward, head tossing, or twitching his ears when something makes him uneasy. This is your cue to slow down and give him time to examine the situation while you reassure him that all is well. Remember the long view: You are not just dealing with this one scary object, you are teaching him how to handle similar situations in the future.

either try to run away, or he will jump toward you for support. When the environment allows, I have the best success with circling the colt until he settles down and then facing him towards the "monster" until he will accept it. It may be necessary to repeat this several times before your horse will face his fear. He will look to you to see if it is really a

threat, so remain calm and set a good example. A calm and soothing tone of voice will help him settle.

There will be times when a young horse will be either rambunctious or rebellious, and he can easily drag or knock you around. I've been knocked over and dragged several times. Mingo pulled me off my feet once when he was only six months old, so don't think a young horse can't do it just because he's small. Always make sure your hands and fingers are not in any loops. I check every few minutes when leading or longeing a horse.

Placing a chain *over* the young horse's nose may not prevent his outbursts, but it will give you more leverage to deal with them and really helps to keep him from pulling away or rearing. Don't put the chain *under* his chin because that will encourage him to rear up to get away from the pressure.

If there is reason to reprimand your horse, give a short tug on the lead and release. Repeat as necessary. Just as when riding with a bit, a steady pull on the halter gives a horse something to brace against, but he can't pull against intermittent tugs. (A sharp word or a loud noise also works with some horses.)

Thread the chain through the lower left-hand ring of the halter, over his nose, through the lower right-hand ring and hook it to top ring on that side. If the chain is threaded over the noseband instead of under it, its jerk will not be as severe. Placing the chain above the noseband will keep it from slipping too low on the colt's nose where it could cut into the tender cartilage.

Your walks with the youngster offer great opportunities to practice leading. Leading a horse in the safe confines of home means little if he won't lead well with the distractions in different environments. After all, that's when good leading

The chain should go over the top of the noseband.

skills are the most important. There will be times when he will probably try your patience. Be patient; your baby will improve. It happens so gradually that, all of a sudden, you will find your horse is a well-behaved companion.

Teach the basics at home, but refine them on your excursions. You should teach your colt the commands of Walk, Trot, Whoa and Stand. He should be able to turn in both directions while maintaining the proper distance from you, regardless of which side you are working from.

A young horse may get excited when he goes out into the world. If you turn him out to play before taking him on his lessons, he will be a little calmer and pay closer attention.

The single most irritating problem I had with Mingo as we were going through this phase of training was his mouthiness. He was constantly grabbing at the chain, the lead rope, or me. This went on for a long time before I found a good solution. I learned to grab his lip and pinch it. After about a month, he finally realized that if he left me, the lead rope and the chain alone, his lip would be left alone, but he would still try it with anyone who was not firm with him.

In time, your horse will become more confident, and when he does get scared he will look to you for support and leadership. At the same time, he will treat you with respect. By the time you are ready to start riding him, your horse will be much better behaved on trail than if you ignore this valuable learning period in his life.

PONYING

If you are fortunate to have a well-trained adult horse, you can teach your baby to pony. Ponying is simply leading one horse while riding another, and it has a great many benefits. It's an excellent way to exercise two horses at one time, and it enables you to work the youngster at a trot, which is difficult if you are leading. A good riding horse will instill confidence in the youngster when encountering new situations. The young horse becomes accustomed to seeing a person above him, as he will when the day comes to ride him. Plus, there is always the chance that, in an emergency, your horse may need to be led by another rider because you are not able to ride or lead him; it will help if this is not new to him. Another possible benefit is that someday in the future the tables may be turned, and your current youngster will be the "older experienced horse." At that time, it will be easy for him to learn his new job.

The only absolute necessity for ponying your horse is a thick cotton lead rope that is easy to grip and that won't do much damage if it is pulled through your hands. A Western saddle is useful because you can dally the rope (don't tie it!) around the horn for more leverage. Beware of getting your fingers crushed between the rope and the horn. A good pair of gloves will help protect your hands from rope burns. Many people pony from an English saddle with no problems, and I suggest trying it before going out to buy a Western saddle just for ponying.

The best place to start is in a round pen, if you have one. If you do not, use the smallest enclosed area big enough to ride in. An assistant should lead the colt on the off side while you lead him on horseback with a second rope from the near side. Gradually take more control until the assistant is doing no more than walking by the colt's side. After a few laps without incident, the assistant

Do's and Don'ts of Ponying:

- Don't consider ponying the colt until he has the proper groundwork. He should be walking, trotting and stopping well, all with a quiet attitude.

- Do keep your colt's head one to two feet away from your right knee.

- Don't let your rope get too long. Your colt may lag behind, and you will lose control.

- Do beware of loops, and watch that your fingers don't get caught between the horn and the rope.

- Don't tolerate any misbehavior from your mount. You will have your hands full enough with the baby.

- Do correct all misbehaviors from the baby. If he crowds, point your toe into his shoulder. Other disciplines that may be necessary are slaps with an open hand or short jerks with the lead rope. A chain over his nose may be helpful.

- Do use a lot of praise for both horses when things are going well.

should disconnect her lead rope and let you go on your own. If all goes well, pick up the pace to a trot.

Include in your training a lot of transitions from a walk to a trot and back. If you use voice commands while doing this, your baby will learn them very quickly. Of course, the most important command to teach is "whoa." The big advantage of doing this while ponying is that the older horse is following the commands and showing the younger horse what to do. In no time at all your baby will respond as fast as, or even faster than, the older horse. Repeat this lesson for several days until the colt is responding well. The next step is to do the same in a larger arena until all are comfortable with the exercises. After that, you can take your young horse almost anywhere.

CHAPTER TWELVE

The First Trail Rides

You have ridden your colt a few times, and you feel he is ready to go out into the big world. Maybe you have acquired an adult horse that has never been ridden on a trail, and you want to try him out. If you prepared your horse with the steps in the previous chapter, it will not be difficult to transition to riding. A horse prepared as described in the previous chapters can be ridden almost immediately on trail. Mingo went on his first trail ride on the fifth ride, and he was quiet and well-behaved. All the miles we had traveled together for those two-plus years before paid off.

Regardless of your preparation, the first trail rides may try your patience and jangle your nerves. Cruiser was such a naturally skittish colt that my early rides on him were downright terrifying. Don't give up—it will get better. I met a woman who had a nineteen-year-old Quarter Horse that she had owned since he was two. Long ago she had taken him on a ride in the park. He got scared, bolted, spun around and ran home, and she never tried again. The woman didn't have any aspirations for showing so for seventeen years she did no more than ride the horse in the arena. When I met her, she was so bored with arena riding that she typically just longed the horse for exercise. Just think of all the pleasurable rides she (and her horse) missed!

When introducing your horse to trail riding, remember this theory behind all training. Learning will not take place if your horse is confused or upset. Your goal is to keep your horse comfortable with his surroundings and secure in his reliance on your judgment. He can then pay attention to what you want him to do.

SPOOKING

The most difficult part of the early rides involves spooking. Of course, if your horse has already seen most of the scary things while you were leading or ponying, the spooks are greatly minimized. One way to stack the cards in your favor is to accompany a friend with a well-behaved horse that will reassure your youngster. However, don't be put off if you don't have someone to ride with. Your horse will look to you for security, just as he did when you were leading him.

When I began riding three-year-old Cruiser in the park I didn't have a riding partner. To help out, since he was a very excitable and spooky horse, I brought my sister along (on foot) on the early rides. I put a halter over Cruiser's bridle and attached a lead rope that was tied around

An interesting method of training involves imagining how you would teach your horse to perform the behavior you are actually trying to correct. For example, you see a backpacker on the road ahead—how would you encourage your horse to spook at the person? Well, you could draw your breath in sharply and hold it, tense your body, lean forward, pull on the reins and scream. To really clinch the deal, hit him with your crop just as he begins to react. Okay…now that you've seen how to get him to spook, reverse your actions to get him to do the opposite. Breathe deeply and calmly, relax your body, sit in your normal riding position with light rein contact and murmur sweet nothings in your horse's ear.

Angel, a three-year-old Quarter Horse can be a little unpredictable. Sue is getting a little help from a friend. Photo by Erin Smith.

his neck. My sister walked alongside and in a crisis she would grab the lead rope until Cruiser calmed down. He usually relaxed before I did. Ellen helped me get through those early rides as much as she helped Cruiser.

As you near a potential spook, try to relax and breath regularly. A horse knows if you are holding your breath and will become frightened because he senses that you are scared. Holding your breath causes tension in your body, which also communicates to your horse that there is something to fear. Instead, develop the habit of exhaling and simultaneously letting your muscles relax whenever you get into a precarious situation. Then talk to the horse in a matter-of-fact voice that not only calms him down, but also keeps you breathing. My sister sings when she gets nervous. Do anything that works well for you and your horse. The worst thing you can do is hold your breath, clamp your reins tightly in your hands, grab with your legs, and lean forward. (Remember, leaning forward tells your horse to go faster—think of jockeys.) Un-

fortunately, this is the instinctive thing to do under such circumstances, so it may take some work to change your habits.

If you are riding with a companion, allow her to go first. Follow with light contact on the reins. If your horse is scared, try to stop him and let him get a good look at the object of his fear. Encourage him reach forward and sniff the object. Allow him to paw at it if pawing will do no harm; this is his way of feeling it. If the "monster" is a human being, greet the person in such a way that you will get a verbal response so your horse will know it is just a person. He will probably relax when he hears a voice.

Do not to continue on your way until your horse becomes visibly comfortable with the situation. This may seem to take a lot of time, but it teaches your horse to face his fears, to investigate, and to trust your judgment. Also, it will make him much less likely to spook in similar situations in the future. He will begin to depend on your judgment if you consistently prove to him that what you tell him is safe really is safe.

If it can be done safely, allow your horse to investigate things that frighten him. This is the first time Mingo ever saw this rock. Photo by Kevin Curry.

Of course, there are always imponderables surrounding horses. One day, I was leading Cruiser up the trail with my nine-year-old niece on his back. It was her first trail ride. There was a log across the trail, and right in front us was a mare that refused to step across it. A number of horses had already passed her, but she wouldn't follow them. Her owner was patient and kept trying in a gentle manner. We crossed over the log and headed down the trail. My sister-in-law was following on foot some distance behind us with my other niece, who was only five. The child scrambled over the log. The mare watched her go and then finally stepped over the log herself. Who knows why she wouldn't follow a horse but she would follow a small child?

If the scary item is something you must pass or cross over, the main point to remember is that you do not want a confrontation. A horse that is petrified may not be able to complete the obstacle on that day. Don't think you are losing if you turn your horse away from the object and work the problem out the next time you ride. You didn't lose. Your horse got as close as he mentally could, and that makes you the winner. Each time afterward, he will be able to get a little closer, until he is finally through.

When you do leave the area, however, make your horse work at a good extended trot if the terrain allows it. This will show him that it's not comfortable to leave the scene of a problem, and that he has to work if you turn back.

The next time you approach the object, try approaching it at an angle so your horse can see it differently. The buddy system is very helpful, too. Horses are so much braver if someone else will go first. A horse that trusts you a lot may feel it is safe if you go first, so try getting off and leading him. This almost always works with Cruiser, but not necessarily with Mingo.

There is nothing wrong with a horse being afraid of an object; fear is normal in any animal. What is essential is to keep your horse from panicking. By avoiding a serious confrontation, you can keep panic out of the picture. Once the horse accomplishes your goal, whatever that might be, do not make him do it over and over for you that day. He made a supreme effort to overcome his fear in order to do what you wished. Praise him for his courage and wait until the next ride to tackle the object again.

If startled from behind, a horse will probably dash forward. Quick reflexes on your part are vitally important in this situation to prevent a runaway. Take the reins in one hand. With your free hand, reach down the rein close to the bit and,

Mingo wasn't so frightened by the wagon once I got off to lead him by it. Photo by Kevin Curry.

using leverage, pull his head to the side, causing him to spin around and face the spook. (This must be done in the first stride or two to be effective. If you allow your horse to gain too much speed, the act of spinning could cause him to fall.) Once you are facing the spook, continue as described before.

This maneuver also works well when your horse is startled by something ahead and spins around to run from it. You merely spin him right back. My incredibly spooky Cruiser was handled this way and eventually he got to the point where, if something scares him from behind, he automatically turns around to see it.

It is important to remember that after your horse has spooked, you need to put the episode out of your mind and move on. If you concentrate on it, you will create tension in your body, which can keep your horse from relaxing and possibly even induce him to spook again. Remember that your horse looks to you for confidence. He will quickly notice any fear on your part.

The stickiest situation on a green horse is a moving spook, usually a motor vehicle. If you hear something coming

that you think will scare your horse, turn and face it as if it was a stationary spook. As it passes, let him watch it, turning him as the monster goes by to keep him looking at it. Whenever it is practical, ask him to follow it. Nothing removes fear faster from a horse than being able to chase what he is afraid of. I've used this technique so often when encountering deer that now I can ride right into a herd without a problem.

I was heading home on Cruiser one day, and across the street a troop of ROTC men were jogging, chanting and carrying a banner. My little horse went crazy, but I turned him around and let him follow them at a brisk trot. He became so enthusiastic with the game that I had a lot of trouble turning him back around to go towards home. A few years later, I had no trouble riding him right through a troop of one hundred soldiers that were marching on our trail.

If you find yourself in a situation where you feel the horse may jeopardize both your lives, such as fearing your horse may jump into the path of a vehicle, by all means, dismount and hold him. Usually, a rider has more control of the horse in the saddle, but sometimes she will personally be safer on the ground. Try to get your horse to stand still when you hop off and be sure that the object is still far enough away that he won't spook while you are in mid-air. One time I waited too long to decide if I should dismount or not, and my horse spun while I was half-off and knocked me off my feet. My hand somehow got twisted in the reins; he dragged me until he got loose and started running toward home. Someone caught him and brought him back to me. I rode home with one hand. I still have a misshapen finger to remind me of my poor judgment.

While it's not a bad idea to practice leaping off your horse to insure your

A BIT OF ADVICE

A full cheek or D-ring snaffle won't hurt your young horse's mouth as badly as a curb bit and it won't slip through his mouth the way some snaffles do. Even a big-ringed, egg butt snaffle can slide into a horse's mouth. If you are using a snaffle that has a round ring, use a dropped, figure-eight, or flash noseband to prevent the bit from pulling through. You can also purchase a rubber or neoprene bit guard that fit between your horse's mouth and the bit ring. These work as stoppers to keep the bit where it belongs. The neoprene guards are easier to slip onto a bit that has large rings. Also, warming the bit inserts in warm water first will make them more pliable.

Personally, I feel that all trail horses are best in a snaffle. If a horse wants to run away, he will run away with any bit you use. If you are starting a horse from scratch, there is absolutely no reason to use any bit other than a snaffle. If you have any doubts about how powerful your snaffle bit is, try this test. Put your foot up on a chair or stool, and drape the headstall of the bridle on your knee so the bit lies on the front of your lower leg. Now pull the reins. That is the pressure the horse feels in his mouth. Imagine what that would feel like in your mouth instead of on your leg.

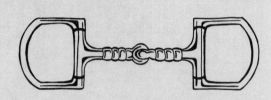

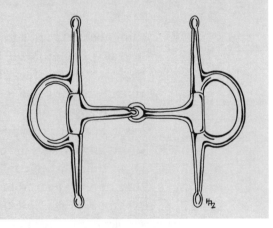

Examples of a D-ring and a full cheek snaffle bit.

A snaffle bit exerts the same amount of pressure on the horse's mouth that you use to pull on the reins. A curb bit uses leverage: Depending on the length of shank, the pressure in your horse's mouth is higher than the amount of pull on the reins. Take a curb bit and run another experiment. Attach the curb chain around the back of your leg, adjusted the way it would be on your horse, and pull the reins. Is it really necessary to have that much pressure on your horse's mouth and jaw? If a snaffle will work, stick with it.

ability to land on your feet (the flying dismount discussed in the next chapter), staying in the saddle can be the better decision! One day, when a pack of motorcycles approached me, I jumped off, misstepped and rolled onto the ground. My horse just looked down at me, and I swear I heard him laugh! He never even looked at the motorcycles.

Many spooks can be avoided by just allowing your horse to look around. There isn't much need for a tight rein if you are alert enough to take contact quickly in an emergency. When I was training my first green horse, we spent

hours walking up and down the street to get used to the traffic. He became very good about it on the lead rope. Imagine my surprise when I started riding him and he spooked at nearly every vehicle that approached from behind. I was baffled for several weeks. Why would he be so different when I was in the saddle? Finally, it dawned on me: When I led him, it was with a loose lead, and he was able to bend his head enough to see traffic approaching from behind him. When I rode, however, I kept the reins just short enough that his movement was impaired. He couldn't get a good look at

Ellen is allowing Mingo to partially turn and examine a worrisome noise behind them.

things behind him, and this made him nervous. The problem went away immediately when I lengthened the reins enough that he could move his head to see a car approaching from the rear. The lesson here is that you need to examine closely any changes in your own behavior or riding when confronting a puzzling new behavior from your horse.

Another method that can help a spooky horse is to apply herd tactics. In the wild, the horses in a herd do not all eat at the same time. There is always at least one horse that is alert and watching for predators. If danger is suspected, he communicates the fact by his body language. His whole posture changes to the familiar high head and pricked ears that horses assume when they are startled. When the other horses see this, they act accordingly. As soon as it is determined there is no danger; the horses resume their relaxed positions.

After you have gained your horse's trust, you will be viewed as a member of the herd. You can capitalize on this with great success. Let's say you are riding along and see a deer close to your trail. Instead of ignoring it and hoping your horse won't see it, literally try to point it out to him. Once he sees it, drop your hand and quietly say, "That's nothing to be afraid of." Then look ahead and move on. In your horse's mind, you are alerting him, determining everything is safe and telling him to ignore it, just by changing your posture.

A similar technique can be used if your horse notices a threat before you do. When he becomes alert, you should become alert too. Wait a moment to see if it is indeed safe, then relax your posture and tell him there is nothing to be afraid of. (Be sure not to hold your breath, or he won't believe you. It may sound silly to you, but this is one way horses communicate with each other.) If you ignore your horse when he becomes alert, he will start to fret because you don't see the danger, and it will only compound the problem. Working with your horse's nature will speed up the process of building a true partnership with him and making him a safe trail horse.

BALKING

Another problem you very likely will face is balking. When caught in the early stages, your firmness will readily prevent this from becoming a serious vice. Remain alert. If your horse plants his feet, and you know it is not caused by fear of something up ahead, a quick kick or a sharp tap with the whip in the area around your leg should be enough to get him going again. Chances are, he is balking only because he doesn't know this is not permissible behavior. You are teaching him otherwise. As he proceeds, praise him profusely. You can also circle him as described above for spooking. If the problem persists, refer to the chapter on problem balkers.

CHAPTER THIRTEEN

Further Training

After the first few trail rides, if things are going smoothly, start using your time on the trail to aid in your horse's overall training. Young horses have a lot of pent-up energy which they need to burn before they will behave calmly and listen. Therefore, if my horse will stay at a trot without fighting to go faster, I like to spend the early part of the ride at a trot. In fact, I often allow the horse to trot as fast as he likes, as long as he stays at a trot. Walking simply holds his energy in until he feels like bursting; cantering, on the other hand, seems to multiply his excitement. However, any time your horse is excitable to the point that it causes a problem on the trail, don't be too proud to turn him out, longe him or ride him at the barn before you take him out. Conflict on the trail is not safe, and does not demonstrate to your horse that trail riding is fun.

RATING YOUR HORSE

Once your horse settles down, you can use long stretches of trail to teach him to trot at a steady tempo and speed. *Tempo* refers to the beat of the gait; *speed* involves the lengthening or shortening of his strides. As you feel your mount slow, urge him on with your legs to control his tempo. To increase speed without changing tempo, keep a steady hold on the reins before encouraging him to move with your legs. You will have to experiment until you get a feel for how strongly to use your aids. Each horse will be a little different.

Do not canter on a trail until your horse can trot calmly. This will help prevent a runaway. An ideal place to introduce the canter is a long, uphill slope, where the hill will control the horse's speed and he will be happy to stop to rest at the top. Riding uphill also makes it harder for a horse to buck from the excitement of cantering out in the open.

Any place that has a major obstacle, such as a road, in a short distance would not be a good choice for cantering, since you may need a lot of stopping distance. Wide-open spaces can be tricky, also. Horses often get excited when they see plenty of room in which to run. Avoid cantering in open areas until you've spent some time cantering your colt on the trail and know that he will proceed calmly. Watch the footing. An inexperienced horse may not know how to balance himself at a canter on uneven or slippery footing. Also in the beginning, never

I found it very important to allow Mingo to trot fast to settle down when he was a three-year-old. Photo by Kevin Curry.

Ride alone as well as in groups. Be sure you can control your horse before cantering in wide open areas. Photo © J. C. Leacock Photography.

canter towards home. Your horse may get very excited, go too fast, and be very difficult to stop. These can develop into bad habits. Unless you have a very quiet colt, it is best to introduce cantering towards the barn when you are a sizable distance away from it.

Anytime your horse gets too wound up, drop him down to a slower gait until he calms down. As he proves that he will be sensible, you can gradually canter more.

TRANSITIONS

The trail is a great place to work on transitions. Typically, a horse will respond well to downward transitions going away from home and upward transitions on the way home. Practicing transitions in this way will greatly improve your work in the ring. In no time your cues become incredibly subtle. On the other hand, doing the transitions when your horse doesn't want to do them as willingly teaches obedience. After the transition is made and your horse is going steadily at the speed you want, remain at that gait for awhile as a reward and praise him profusely.

CORNERS

Bending around corners in the same manner as you would when schooling in the arena will reinforce your turning aids. Sure, your horse could go around a corner very easily without you doing a single thing—he'll just follow the trail. However, you would lose a perfect chance to further his education, increase his suppleness and increase his balance. Look for places to practice bending, such as around trees and bushes, and pretend they are cones set up in the

Ellen uses trees as if they were cones.

arena. If your horse can bend around a tree in the open, just think how good he will be when you take him back in the ring!

Sharp corners are also a perfect place to cue your horse for a particular lead. Use it as you would a corner on an arena. It seems more natural in the horse's mind to pick up the correct lead on the trail than in the arena. That is what he'd do if you weren't on his back and he were loose. Soon he will be picking up any lead you request, whether you are going around a corner or down a straight section of trail, and you'll wonder how he could learn so quickly. I always make it a point of fine-tuning the canter leads so I am able to canter on the right lead, trot two steps, canter on the left lead, trot two steps, and so on. This can all be taught without even seeing a fence.

NECK REINING

You can easily teach your horse to neck rein while trail riding. Even if you ride English, you will never regret taking the time to do this. Many times on the trail you will want to ride with one hand, freeing the other hand to do something else. During the bug-infested summer months when I ride at a walk, I always have the reins in one hand so the other can kill the bugs that land on my horse's neck. In the cold winter months, riding with large, warm gloves is easier if you can neck rein. I usually alternate hands and keep one on the reins and the other in my pocket. A side benefit to riding with a neck rein is that you very easily can scratch your horse's withers as a reward.

Neck reining is also useful if you have somehow injured a hand, wrist or arm and cannot use one of your hands to hold a rein. When I smashed my finger, I was grateful I spent the time teaching my horse to neck rein. I was a long way from home when it happened. I was also able to ride during the week it took for my finger to heal.

All that you have to do to teach your horse to neck rein is use the outside rein on a turn or corner as you would a neck rein, while at the same time using the inside rein as a direct rein. Use your legs and weight in the same manner as always. If you do this all the time, your horse will learn the neck rein without any concentrated training. Work on it when you do ring work to reinforce the concept. Neck reining doesn't require a curb bit—it can easily be done with a snaffle. If there are any English riders who are still opposed to this "western riding" idea, keep in mind that the indirect reining that more advanced dressage riders do is nothing more than a neck rein with a different name.

DISCIPLINE

As a responsible rider, you—not your horse—are the one to decide where to go and at what speed. Your mount thus learns to accept discipline and follow precise aids. Being firm in his early training will pay off a hundredfold in later years. While it may seem harsh not to allow him to do the things he wants to during a ride, you are explaining to him the rules that he should follow the rest of his life. At some time or another, you will have to lay down the law, and it is far better to do it before bad habits are instilled and harsh measures have to be taken.

RIDING ALONE

Your early rides should, if possible, be with an older, quiet horse, but as you and your horse become confident, be sure to make the effort to ride him by yourself. Every barn I've ever been to seems to have at least one horse that cannot be ridden alone. His rider is always waiting for someone else to show up so

I once had a horse whose previous owners allowed him to run up hills whenever he wanted. What horse doesn't love doing that? It's an easy habit to start. He would go up hills at breakneck speed, particularly if we were going towards home. I could only hope that no one was ahead of us around a bend. At one point after an injury to his leg, I actually had to avoid part of the trail because I didn't want him to harm himself by dashing up a hill. Make sure your horse knows that you are the one who determines when, where, and how fast you will travel. It could save you or him from a bad accident.

she can ride, and both horse and rider are missing many wonderful rides. A situation like this can be prevented by going out on your own as soon as your horse is safe and ready. This way, he doesn't learn to rely on the herd; rather, he learns to rely on his rider.

GROUP RIDES

Riding in large groups can be more difficult than riding alone. Try to ride in small groups when training your horse. Work on good group behavior in these small groups of two or three, and then gradually move to larger groups as your horse becomes more experienced and trustworthy.

Your horse should be accustomed to riding in all positions of the group: front, middle and back. Working in the lead in small doses, plus doing a lot of riding alone, will encourage a timid leader. A friend of mine had an Arabian mare named Krystal. It took nearly a whole summer before that horse would take the lead position, and then it was only on the way home. The first time Krystal took the lead for a few feet, she received a lot of praise. Each time after that she would keep the lead a little longer until, at last, she was able to lead all the way.

A far more difficult problem is the horse that insists on being the leader. Once again, it is good to start in small groups of just one or two other horses. Do the initial work at a walk where it is hard for your horse to pass, and praise him profusely.

If your horse tries to crowd or pass another horse, stop and make him back up for a few steps, then move forward again. Repeat this each time he speeds up. Or if there is space, try riding in a circle alongside the group and then drop back onto the trail. Pulling your horse to the side will distract him, but will not cause the same type of confrontation that stopping or turning away might.

Gradually work up to some short stretches of trotting. Ask your companions to keep up a good speed so your horse will follow without too much work on your part to keep him from passing. The hardest gait to control, of course, is the canter. I've found it helpful to start with a sizable distance between your horse and the horse ahead of you. This will, once again, make it more difficult for your horse to pass the others. Avoid situations where a horse that wants to lead can race other horses; it

Don't allow your horse to get in a "race" with another horse. Photo © K. S. Swigart.

will only encourage the tendency. As your horse improves, gradually begin riding in larger groups and placing your horse further in the back.

Other training to work on in groups include slowing or stopping your horse while the group continues on, leaving the group and quietly catching up with them once again, maintaining proper distance between horses, and just plain good manners with other horses.

MOUNTING

Probably the most vulnerable moment when riding a horse is in the midst of mounting. You are off-balance, not in firm control of the horse, and moving between the two secure positions of being on the ground and atop the horse. Your horse should stand still for mounting. Practice this both at home and on the trail. Some horses are fine in a ring, but won't stand when they have a lot of space around them. Step up into the stirrup and ask your horse to stand. If he moves, return your free leg to the ground and restrain him until he is quiet. Then try again. Be sure to praise him when he shows any sign of improvement.

Don't fall for the temptation of letting your horse graze while you mount. It is unsafe and looks sloppy and unprofessional. A horse should not be allowed to graze when he has a bit in his mouth. Besides, if your horse has a long rein when you mount, what will you do if he gets spooked? You will have no control at all. When your reins are shorter you can gather them up quickly and take action.

There are several ways to discourage a horse that insists on moving about while you mount him. One way is by making him move. Move him in circles, backwards and sideways. Horses do not like this and will eventually figure out that standing still is the easier and more pleasant option. Some horses only need their heads bent sharply to the side until they settle down. Once your horse is willing to stand, return his head to the normal position as a reward.

If your horse won't stand still for mounting in the arena at home, you certainly can't expect him to behave on trail. Make a conscious effort to practice good mounting all the time. At the end of an arena lesson, ask your horse to stand still. Dismount and immediately mount again. Do this as many times as necessary until you notice some improvement or your legs get too tired. Mounting sloppily due to tired legs will not encourage your horse to stand quietly. Give him lots of praise for good behavior and call it quits as the ultimate reward.

You can do this while on the trail, too. As you approach home, turn your horse in the opposite direction and practice dismounting and mounting. Facing your horse in the direction away from home before you mount may make more willing to cooperate. As soon as he stands, dismount, loosen the girth and lead him the rest of the way home.

Although you should always mount with precision, taking care not to pull the saddle sideways, toe your horse's belly or kick him in the back as you swing your leg over, a good trail horse should be accustomed to all those things. The last thing you need is for your horse to get spooked while you are mounting him ten miles from home.

If you think that you are the perfect mounter and will always be able to mount with precision, imagine mounting after a bad fall where you may have been injured. A twisted ankle will not allow you to jump, a sore back interferes with precision, and an injured hand will not let you get a good grip. Make sure your horse knows how to

View training as offering your horse two options. One is the easy and pleasant thing you want him to do; the other is a little uncomfortable and involves work. The latter is not punishment. Your horse will soon amaze you with his wise choices.

One of the strangest bits of luck I've ever seen took place on a beautiful spring day. My sister had gotten off her horse, Ranger, to lead him over an obstacle. As she was going to mount, she felt a sneeze coming and paused. She knew it wouldn't be safe to mount as she was sneezing. I was wondering about the delay when suddenly we heard a crack. Startled, we looked up to see a tree about fifty feet away come crashing to the ground. Ranger jumped, and my horse took off. Fortunately, he bolted away from home, so I was able to stop him fairly quickly. If that tree had fallen while my sister was in the midst of mounting, she could have been seriously injured. Saved by a sneeze!

A good trail horse, like Ranger, will stand even if he gets kicked while being mounted.

When I first heard this suggestion, I was skeptical, imagining that if you gave a horse this kind of warning, he would try to prevent you from mounting. However, as I've used this technique, I have found that the horses don't do that at all—rather, they slowly improve.

If you have a tall horse or have difficulty mounting at home, teach your horse to stand quietly beside a log, stump, or fence to make mounting easier. Teach your horse to move precisely where you want and stand there for mounting. It will come in handy many times as you trail ride.

STANDING

One of the most useful things you can teach a horse is to stand still when he is not tied or being held. The cowboys call this *ground tying*. You will never regret the time taken to teach this lesson. You can start teaching your horse when he is very young, long before you ride

stand correctly first, then practice mounting in a sloppy manner at home so your horse will get used to standing quietly regardless of the way you mount. Also, make sure to train your horse to allow you to mount from either side.

Sometimes, particularly if he is very young, a horse will take a step or two when you mount because he is thrown off balance. It helps to give him a warning that you want to mount by tugging firmly on the stirrup or cantle. This clues your horse to brace himself first. He may need to take a step to rebalance, so allow him to do that.

him, just by asking him to stand while you are leading or longeing him at the barn. Hold on to your rope and correct him with a tug whenever he takes a step. Use a command like "stand" or "stay." Reward him when he is good, both with verbal praise and by rubbing his neck or withers—whatever you know he likes.

Gradually increase the time he stands and the distance you are from him. As he gets better, walk around to his sides and behind him. I slap the rope gently on his sides, sacking him out for ropes at the same time I am teaching him to stand. If he takes a step, immediately return him to the spot where you asked him to stand.

Be sure to shed your own anxieties and hyperactivity before trying to teach this lesson. Your goal is to show him that standing still is easy—much easier than working—and that relaxing and just hanging out are quite pleasant. You cannot do this if you are wound up and tense. No matter what you intend your words and actions to tell him, your body will be saying something different.

Do not let your horse graze; that means he is not paying any attention to you. In any event, you don't want your horse to eat with a bit in his mouth. Eventually, you can disconnect the lead rope and ask him to stand without controlling him. If he does take a step, grab his halter and return him to his spot.

Once he is good at standing with you beside him, ask your horse to stand in one spot in an arena and leave him alone in there. Leave him for longer and longer periods each time. This should always be at the very end of a training session, so he gets a great reward for good behavior—quitting for the day. Even better, unsaddle him during the stand and then turn him free in the arena so he can have some time to himself. This also teaches him to allow you to adjust or remove his tack while he remains still. There have been a few times on the trail when I had to completely remove the saddle and replace it with my horse untied. This is an easy task on a horse that has been trained to stand.

Introduce standing loose on the trail gradually. At first, stay within arm's reach and stand between your horse and home. If your mount decides to go anywhere, it will be towards home, and you will be able to reach out and grab him. The only way he will learn ground tying is with praise—punishment will get you nowhere.

As his ability to stand increases, teach your horse to stand quietly, untied, while you pick up his feet to check for stones. Many horses only get their feet cleaned when they are tied up or in the small confines of a stall. It can be extremely frustrating if your horse goes lame on the trail and there nobody to hold him while you check his feet. The forelegs are easy because you can hold the reins, but the hind legs can be tough. Start on this task at home in the round pen, using a halter, lead rope and, if necessary, a chain over the nose. Tell your horse to stand and reach down to pick up his foot. If he moves, reprimand him with your voice and a quick tug on the lead rope.

Many people say you should always pick up a horse's feet in a certain order so that he learns the habit and will lift his feet more willingly as you go around. However, you don't want to have to lift up all his feet simply to get to the one you want—that would be silly. Teach your horse to lift any foot at random. Work with him until you can get him to lift each foot without moving out of position. Then do it while out on the trail. He will probably stand just fine.

A horse must also learn to stand still on command while you are on his back. You can accomplish this by being firm and persistent. Approach it the same way as for the horse that won't stand for mounting. That is, move him about in uncomfortable ways, and then ask him to stand. Standing still will become a very appealing choice for him.

When training, I ask my horse to stop and stand for a few moments when we are a few hundred feet from home. If he is good, I will then dismount, loosen the girth and lead him home. Stopping and standing thus results in a great reward. The standing duration can be increased; soon he won't care how long he stands.

It is useful to teach your horse to stand still on a loose rein. This is essential

Cruiser is standing still while I clean his foot. Photo by Ellen Daly.

The sergeant of the mounted patrol unit in our park suggests that you poke your horse with your finger or the end of a pen on the withers or neck if he is dancing about. As soon as he stops dancing, you stop poking. You have given him a very good reason to stand still. A horse that can feel a fly land on his neck can certainly feel a pen gently poking. Although I haven't had the opportunity yet to try this, I imagine that the technique works; after all, the unit's horses stand quietly in one spot for great lengths of time.

Instead of pulling the reins to get her horse to stand still, Penny would be better off circling Trooper, the Tennessee Walker, until he settles down.

If your horse stands quietly, you can adjust your stirrups while mounted as Ellen is doing here. Photo © John Burkett.

soon as he is standing. Keep doing this until the horse realizes how much more comfortable it is to stand quietly without rein contact. Do not try this on the trail, however, until your horse is reliable at home.

You can also teach a horse to stop and stand when someone falls off. Begin this at home by first practicing the flying dismount. It is safer for the rider to learn this maneuver at a slow gait. Start the dismount at a slow walk and as the horse learns to stop, increase the speed to a trot. I've never been daring enough to try it at a canter, but if you are braver than I am and very athletic, you can give it a try.

While you are riding, take your feet out of the stirrups, put your hands on the withers or the front of the saddle for balance, and leap off. As you land on the ground (hopefully, on your feet) ask your horse to stop and stand. Praise him when he does. Practice this out on the trail once your horse dependably stops in the ring and you are good at landing. A side benefit of this is that your horse also will stand better when you mount him.

A really smart horse will learn to stop as soon the rider takes her feet out of the stirrups. This is good, too. If you accidentally lose a stirrup, he may slow down or stop and give you a chance to pick it back up. This could prevent a fall. Although your horse may be too scared or excited to stop if you fall off on the trail, these lessons are still worth teaching. He just might remember, saving you a long hike home.

TOUCHING

A young horse may be skittish with a rider moving about on his back. You should accustom your horse to having

if you want to be able to adjust your tack from the saddle. The length of the stirrups for an English saddle can be adjusted without ever dismounting. You may also need to adjust your saddlebags or your own clothing. I make my horses stand while I put on gloves. When doing these things, you can't have a tight hold on the reins.

Start teaching your horse to stand with a loose rein by gradually lengthening the rein. If your horse tries to step away, pull up the rein quickly. Release as you bend over on his neck and turn your body around in the saddle. It won't be long before the time comes that it will be necessary to do this, so you might as well begin early. There are many times you will have to duck a branch, reach around for something, or brush off an obnoxious insect. Start working at this cautiously and praise your horse for good behavior. At the same time, teach your horse to accept you touching any part of his body while you are mounted, including his face and ears where insects can be the worst.

VOICE COMMANDS

Although many young horses already know voice commands by the time they are ridden, it is good to reinforce these when you are on the trail. The show horse must learn to respond to the commands of physical aids and not depend on a rider's voice, but a trail horse that will respond to a voice command without any other aids is very handy if you accidentally drop your reins, lose your stirrup or get injured on a ride and cannot use other aids properly. It also is simply convenient. I train all the horses I ride to transition to a lower gait when I exhale loudly.

It is easy to teach voice commands on the trail because you can ride so many miles and do so many transitions. It doesn't seem like work or drudgery. All you have to do is use your voice every time you use the physical aid, and soon the horse will understand very well. You can teach him any words you like.

As I demonstrate on Cruiser, the flying dismount is a maneuver you should practice at home before you attempt to do it on the trail. Photo © John Burkett.

Spend the time to accustom your young horse to being touched all over while you are in the saddle. Photo by Ellen Daly.

A picnic table is a great barrier to use to teach a horse to back up. Ranger understands much better if Ellen positions him in front of it and asks him to back up.

Brush your jacket on your horse's body to completely desensitize him to it. Mingo hardly cares at all. Photo by Ellen Daly.

BACKING

Always reinforce the backing command that you initially school on at home. A great time to do this is right before you turn around to go home or right before you arrive at home or the trailer. Ask your horse for a good solid stop, back a few steps and then turn around or get off. Your horse gets one of those ultimate rewards that make such a wonderful impression on him.

You can also take advantage of obstacles you find on the trail to encourage your horse to back. Use a fence, hedge or even a picnic table to block his path. It makes sense to a horse to back when he is facing something that keeps him from going forward.

Once your horse stops and backs away from an obstacle, stop him randomly along the trail and ask him to back. Hopefully, he will take a few steps backwards, and you can then praise him and go on your way. Don't ask for the same number of steps each time. Sometimes ask for two; sometimes five, and so on. This prevents him from getting into a routine and assuming that he will always move forward after four steps.

TURN ON THE HAUNCHES

When your horse is good at backing, you can teach him to turn on his haunches. Turning on the haunches is a move during which the horse turns around with his front legs without moving his hind legs. This maneuver is particularly useful for turning on a narrow trail, and all trail horses should know it. They don't have to do it so well that they would earn a ribbon in the show ring—just well enough to be functional.

To turn your horse to the left, use an obvious leading left rein, a neck rein on the right and a strong right (outside) leg behind the girth. Prevent the horse from going forward with your reins. On a narrow trail the maneuver will make sense to a horse. In an arena, he probably won't understand it as quickly. Asking for a turn on the haunches when turning homeward gives your horse a lot of incentive and the great reward. Teach your horse to do the turn in both directions. Each time he obeys, lighten the cues until finally all you will need is a light leg and a neck rein.

If a horse just can't seem to keep from advancing forward when you ask for the turn on the haunches, try turning him with a fence or other obstacle in front, as suggested for backing.

LATERAL MOVEMENTS

A handy horse must be able to move from one side of the trail to the other promptly and at any gait. All too often

You can start teaching your colt to move laterally from the ground before you ride him, and this will speed his learning. Standing on one side of your horse, use your hand to apply pressure on his side where your heel would go if you were mounted. Be sure to keep his head straight. Increase the pressure if he doesn't move. You can use an obstacle to block forward progress, as suggested for teaching backing and turning on the haunches.

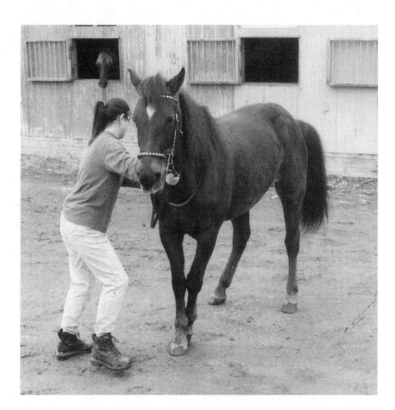

Ellen is teaching Ranger to sidepass from the ground by applying pressure to the area where her foot touches his side.

branches, mud, ice or other obstacles suddenly appear and must be bypassed. Maybe your horse is traveling too close to the edge of the trail and you don't want to bang your knee on the tree coming up (a very painful occurrence).

It is fairly easy to teach your horse to move sideways. Suppose you are on the left side of the trail and want to go to the right. You want him to move from the pressure of your left leg. Start small, using only a little extra pressure with that leg. Chances are, he will ignore you. At this point, tap your calf on his side; use your right rein as a direct rein, your left rein against his neck, and shift your whole body over in the direction you want him to go. His natural response is to correct this imbalance by moving his body in the same direction. All the other aids will encourage him to make that decision. When he takes a step or two in the right direction, cease your aids and reward him with lots of praise. In a few minutes, try it again. Of course, always teach the sidepass in both directions.

Gradually, you can eliminate the other aids and lighten the leg aid. Soon you will be able to zigzag your horse back and forth down the trail at all gaits with the lightest of aids. You will also find that it has become easy to keep your horse on the rail when you school him in the arena. Of course, if when on the trail you don't pay close enough attention to what's coming up, your knee will still get banged. I'm given this strong reminder at least once a year.

Some things may come easily for your horse, while it may take many rides before you see any improvement in others. Perseverance and consistency will pay off with even the most difficult horse. With the average horse, if the time and effort were spent early in his training, serious problems should not develop. The difficult problems usually occur when retraining an older horse with bad habits or with a horse that has had a frightening experience on the trail.

CHAPTER FOURTEEN

Retraining the Runaway

Many problem horses have a combination of problems. It may be that your horse is a runaway, but he is only bad on the way home. In that case, he is showing signs of being barn sour. A horse that rears only when you ask him to leave home is also balking. Some prancers are really runaways that are being held back, and horses that refuse to cross water may have balking tendencies. Don't pigeonhole your horse with a label, but read and consider all the scenarios before you attempt to solve his problem behaviors.

The only constant in the horse world is that no rules are engraved in stone. The following suggestions for retraining a difficult horse are just that—suggestions. Every horse, rider and environment will be different. Review carefully the methods given here to see just how they will work for your horse. Some adjustments probably will have to be made. There are many roads to the same destination; these ideas merely give you a map. You may need to take some detours for your particular situation, or you may even discover a shortcut.

RETRAINING THE OLDER HORSE

Retraining an older horse usually poses a far greater challenge than the initial training of a young horse. Very often problems are deeply ingrained and are the result of circumstances of which the trainer is unaware. Unlike the young horse that can be started trail riding very early in his training, the older horse should not be brought out on the trail until the rider is confident of her horse's behavior in an arena.

Some older horses are well-behaved but just haven't been ridden on trail before. They can be treated much like younger, green-broke horses, following the advice in the section on training a young horse. Keep in mind, though, that an older horse may not be as open-minded and accepting as a younger one. Things will appear more frightening to an older horse that has never been ridden on the trail, and this may result in spookiness and balkiness. Patience is the key. Don't rush your horse into doing too much, too soon.

If you are having any problems in the arena (such as bucking, rearing or unwillingness to go forward) they will only be worse out on trail. Solve your problems at home. Teach your horse to be obedient, to trust you and respect you in a safe environment before taking him out into the world.

If your horse leads well, supplement your arena work by taking him for walks.

123

You will be safer on foot than in the saddle. If your horse doesn't lead well, that's a great place to start your training at home. Leading is the first step in a horse's education. If your horse won't lead correctly, it shouldn't surprise you that he has trouble with more advanced things. Many adult horses are lacking in this basic skill, and it shouldn't be neglected in their retraining program.

As he improves in the arena, start leading your horse on short walks around the yard and neighborhood. Some horses get very excited when they leave their safe environment, so be prepared for possible problems. Typically, behavior will be the worst on the way home, so don't go too far at first. Each day, take him on longer and more challenging walks. It is best to do this after your arena ride, when he is tired. He will think of it as a break from training and view it as a reward. It's a great way to start on his attitude adjustment. Soon your horse should look forward to going out on walks away from his barn. Hopefully he will transfer this attitude to trail rides as well.

Not all horses are equal candidates for retraining. A dear friend was very ill and wanted to give my sister her spoiled Appaloosa, Casper. His previous owner had raced him on the trail. The present owner's daughter rode him only in the arena. I had tried trail riding him, and he was a basket case. After a great deal of thought, my sister decided she wasn't experienced enough to deal with the problem. Combined with the fact that she didn't like him very much, it became clear that Casper wasn't worth the risk to her to retrain him.

Eventually, Casper was sold to another woman in our barn who was willing to make the effort to retrain him, and he turned into a fine trail horse. My sister found a much more suitable horse for herself and never regretted her decision.

CAUSES OF THE RUNAWAY

Riding a runaway horse is one of the most terrifying experiences you can ever endure. It's akin to losing the brakes on your car while speeding downhill, heading for a busy intersection, while, at the same time, you only have limited steering abilities! Most people can ride a horse that is going fast, but the fear of what he may run into can petrify a rider. A couple of minutes can seem like an eternity. In the area where I usually ride, the upcoming threat is the intersection of a busy street. In one incident, my horse decided it would be quicker to run down the center of the street, following the yellow line instead of the trail that paralleled it.

Any horse can take off in a panic. This basic instinct goes back to prehistoric times. Due to his flight-or-fight tendency, the horse's first reaction is to run from imminent or imagined danger if he can. Only if trapped will a horse fight to defend himself.

Since all horses are prone to running away, the smart rider will rehearse a plan of action in her mind as to what to do if it happens. Otherwise, she may panic and cause an accident either by the wrong action or by inaction. The only way to keep the number of such incidents down is to expose your horse to many different, potentially frightening environments, get him accustomed to dealing with scary things and teach him to trust your judgment. Even so, my most trusty steed ran away when a small avalanche crashed a scant thirty feet away. It's best to be prepared.

There are three major causes of runaway horses. The first and most common is fear. The average horse will only have a few isolated instances of running away in his career, and most of these will occur in his early days of trail riding. Riding with an experienced horse can help prevent problems. If an old pro is unmoved by something that scares a green horse, the novice horse may not bolt, or do it only half-heartedly and thus be easier to stop.

Another reason a horse runs away is that he is excited and "feeling his oats." He wants to canter and when given the chance, he goes faster and faster and doesn't want to stop. If you are in tune with your horse, you can sense the days he is "in a mood," and reduce the runaway risk by turning him out to play first, longeing before riding, or riding in an arena until he settles down. Once you are out on trail, trot him fast and far until you sense an easing in his excitement level. He may volunteer to canter. Try to catch him on the first stride or two and keep him trotting. A brisk trot will calm a horse down whereas cantering will increase his excitability.

After you feel that the wild edge is wearing off, choose a safe area to canter, and make sure he waits for your command. Ask him for a canter, but be ready to bring him back to a trot if he is showing any signs of losing control. The best place to let him canter is up a long, sloping hill. This will tire him, whereas a short or steep hill will only make him more excited.

The third kind of runaway and, without a doubt, the worst kind, is the horse that has learned he can run away and does so from habit. It doesn't take too many incidents of successful bolting from either fear or excitement for a horse to learn he can get away with it.

My first horse's original owner used to race him on trail when he was only a green-broke two-year-old, and this turned into a habit that affected his trail riding for the rest of his life. Twenty years later I met that owner. In her ignorance, the woman bragged about how she had raced him and how un-

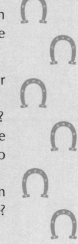

Before you begin retraining a horse with serious trail riding problems, spend some time thinking about the following:

- Is it worth the risk to yourself and your horse to retrain him?
- Do you have the experience for the job?
- Is trail riding so important that you are willing to spend the necessary time to do it right?
- Would you be better off riding only in an arena setting or getting another horse?

Allow a horse that is prone to run away to trot with a loose rein, so he can stretch his legs and enjoy himself.

Trot-canter-trot transitions demonstrate to your horse that you are in control. These are more humane than the solution most people suggest: a stronger bit. Besides, if a horse really wants to run, no bit will stop him. It is much better to *teach* a horse to obey than to try to *force* him to obey.

stoppable he had been. She said she used to carry spare curb chains because he had learned how to twist his jaw and break them to evade the bit. Needless to say, he also had developed a very hard mouth.

The sad thing is, this woman not only ruined a horse, but also created a lot of unnecessary fear in herself. A friend of mine went riding with her and said they never went faster than a trot because she was afraid her horse might get excited and run away. All these years later, she was still paying for her carelessness, just as I was.

STOPPING THE RUNAWAY

The most common advice given to stop the runaway is to pull the horse's head to the side with one rein and ride him in a circle. Keep decreasing the size of the circle until he is under control. Pulling straight back on the reins when a horse has stiffened his neck or has the bit in his teeth is useless. A circle will naturally slow your horse down.

How do you get a horse that is going top speed (and perhaps in a panicked state of mind) to circle? The first act is to sit back, even though your natural inclination when you are frightened is to lean forward. Leaning forward will only speed him up. After sitting back, loosen your outside rein, shorten your

inside rein and bring it out to the side, pulling with that rein only. It may help to put your outside hand on the saddle or the horse's withers for balance. He will gradually start to turn, and you can then decrease the size of the circle until he stops.

Don't give a steady pull on the rein; rather, you should pull and release. A horse can brace himself against steady pressure, but he has much more difficulty with intermittent pressure. (If you want to test this for yourself, have someone hold one end of a rein while you hold the other. Try to maintain a steady pressure on the rein while your partner also has a steady pressure on the rein, and then ask your friend to pull and release. The difference is amazing.)

It is best to stop a runaway horse on the first stride or two before he gains momentum, just as described in the section on spooking. As he takes the initial leap, grab up one rein very short and loosen the other to spin him 180 degrees. If he is running from fear, the horse will find himself facing the frightful object, and he will certainly not want to run that way. After that, it is just a matter of calming him down. Keep in mind that he is scared and that as soon as you turn him back in the direction in which he originally wanted to run, he may bolt again. Be prepared to circle him again if necessary. If your horse was just trying to run away with you for the fun of it, you have foiled him successfully. After going through this enough times, he may give up on running. Take care with this maneuver, however. If you try to spin him when he is going too fast or the footing is slippery; you could easily cause him to fall.

Circling is great under ideal circumstances, but what do you do on a narrow path that doesn't allow you to

As always, think for the long term, and consider where your actions will lead. I remember one man who bought a Thoroughbred racehorse just off the track. I rode with him down trail in the beginning, and his horse wasn't too bad for an adult on his first trail rides. This man had every reason to expect his horse to become a fine trail horse in a few months. But then he unwisely allowed the horse to trot up the hill alongside the road right before the barn. His argument was that it was easier for the horse, and the horse liked it.

After a few weeks of this, the horse wanted to run up the hill. The owner's new argument was, "He always stops at the top." In a few more weeks, I watched from the bottom of the hill as his horse kept running over the top of the hill down the street. He continued to run all the way home. The horse went up for sale the very next week, and the new owner had to work with him for many months before he would walk toward home in a somewhat safe manner. I saw her riding him a few years later, and she was still having problems with him. A few weeks ago I learned the horse was sold yet again—his third owner since he came off the track nine years ago. If the first owner had the foresight to envision where his actions would lead, he would have walked that last stretch of trail home and so many difficulties could have been avoided.

circle? If at all possible, head for a hill that you can run up, and slow your horse down that way. Most people aren't lucky enough to have their horse bolt near a convenient hill, though—I've certainly never been. I have had some good success doing a maneuver similar to a circle: I turn the horse only enough to bend his body sharply, yet not enough to make him run off the path; then I alternate sides back and forth every stride or two. For example, I bend him sharply to the left, gallop a couple of strides, switch my aids and bend him sharply to the right, gallop a few strides and switch back to the left again. Strong leg aids will help to bend him. I keep this up until he slows down, and I don't quit until he drops down into a trot. Again, the reins are pulled and released

Sharon and Beauty are showing how a sharp 180-degree turn within the first couple strides is the best way to stop a runaway horse.

so he has nothing to resist. It takes a little time, but if you can't circle, you really don't have many options.

Sometimes you can stop a horse by being creative. I once slowed a panicked Arabian filly by running her into a river and by the time she got to the other side, she forgot what she was running from. A Quarter Horse mare, startled by some bikes coming around the corner, decided to show me her sprinting capabilities and spun around (on a dime, of course) to run home. I was able to make her take a wide turn around a corner, going off the path and up the side of the road, away from home. She came to a dead stop in just a couple of strides when she realized she was no longer running toward her safe barn.

ARENA TRAINING

Even if the runaway habit has been formed, all is not lost. The best place to start retraining is to go back to the arena or whatever enclosed space you have available and work on the basics. Your horse may be good in the ring and only prone to running away on trail. In this case, spend a lot of time working on all sorts of transitions from one gait to another. Teach him to stop from all gaits. Don't omit training him to back up correctly. Backing teaches a horse to yield to the bit—an essential ingredient in stopping a runaway horse. As usual, use ample praise to encourage good behavior and instill the proper habits permanently in his mind.

Do a lot of calm cantering, and practice slowing down the canter on command. Spend as much time with this as necessary until you are sure he knows it well. At the end of the session, cool him down with a loose rein and allow him to relax.

If your horse is pulling runaway tricks in the arena too, the training program must be adjusted. Start in the smallest possible enclosed area you can find. In time, the horse will realize he has nowhere to run to. My sister once worked with an Arabian mare that had a reputation of bolting anywhere and everywhere. As soon as the horse was mounted in a large arena, she took off like her tail was on fire. It took a couple of laps to stop her, and a few seconds later she did it again. A round pen was available at this stable, so my sister took the horse directly to it. There they had a brisk workout of cantering and trotting with a lot of transitions. Soon, Beauty was dripping with sweat. Eventually, she figured there was no place to run to in a small round pen, and she quit playing her games. After that, she hardly gave her owner any serious problems with bolting in an enclosed area, but it took months of work before she was trustworthy on trail at a canter. Eventually, however, she became an excellent trail horse.

Of course, everyone has to work with the facilities available, so if you don't have a small place to begin your retraining, spend a lot of time working on slow speeds. Do the same when you are ready to move from the small ring into a larger one. Patience will prevail.

Every time you work the horse, concentrate heavily on transitions. Your goal is to teach him that you will decide what gait and speed he will use. Although it may make you feel like a dictator, obedience is absolutely necessary with this kind of horse. Of utmost importance is the lesson that "whoa" means "whoa." Start with the slower gaits and only increase the speed when you are satisfied with his behavior. For example, begin with walk-whoa transitions until the horse is very responsive. At that stage, start intermixing walk-trot transitions. Build up to trot-whoa and canter-whoa transitions. If your horse tries to accelerate without your permission, patiently bring him into a small circle until he settles down. Then try again.

Working in only one small part of the arena will help control his exuberance. In fact, you'll probably get the best results if you work in a circle close to the exit. Be prepared for him to try to race towards the exit when you face it, but on the positive side, this gives you a chance to make it clear that he is not allowed to race against your wishes. As the horse improves, venture away from the gate for longer periods. At least in the early rides, save your cantering for the end of the lesson when your horse is tired and will cooperate better. Also, if he does well, you can quit on a good note, which is a wonderful way to use positive reinforcement.

Before you ever go out on trail with your runaway, be sure you can stop him at all gaits in the arena. As usual, ample praise for good behavior will encourage him to learn quickly.

A spoiled, runaway horse can run away at virtually any gait. My runaway Morgan, Brandy, took off on me a number of times, yet he never got faster than a trot. The runaway often has the mindset that any release of pressure on the reins is an invitation to go faster. Quite often, the rider must have a death grip on the reins to keep her horse at a walk or slow trot. At the slightest easing of rein contact, the horse will speed up a notch. It is fatiguing for the rider, painful for the horse and not the least bit of fun for either. Brandy has caused blisters to sprout on many a rider's fingers. These cases are not hopeless, though. Their behavior can be changed with patience and positive reinforcement.

The perfect time to start changing this headstrong mindset is when you are cooling off your horse. Simply teach him to walk forward calmly on a loose rein. If you start this during a cool-off period, your horse will feel more like walking to begin with. Ask him to walk and immediately slacken your reins when he responds. If he tries to resume a trot, take contact with the reins again and repeat your request. Once again, loosen your reins at the first sign of response. It will probably take quite a bit of repetition, depending on how bad your horse is, but eventually he will find the loose rein so much more comfortable that he will

Teach your trail horse to make smooth transitions on a loose rein in the arena or home pasture just as this pleasure horse is doing. Photos © B. J. McKinney.

welcome it. It will change his whole frame of mind. He will feel that slack rein flapping on his neck and no contact in his mouth, and he'll know it's time to be quiet and relaxed. This behavior will carry through to riding. It may take a little practice until he makes the connection, but he is sure to learn it. Horses much prefer to be relaxed, and a relaxed horse is much more comfortable to ride.

TRAIL TRAINING

At some point, you will be ready to move out into the open. Before you go out on trail, ride in a large pasture or on a long driveway close to the barn, if possible, to help make the arena-trail transition a little smoother.

Use your discretion as to whether your horse will do best with company or alone on trail. Every horse is different. A horse whose problem stems from racing would do less well in a group of horses because he would get excited and want to race. Conversely, a horse that runs because he gets nervous would be calmed down if he were with another horse.

The first few rides should be at a walk. Don't go out too far, even if he is doing well, because chances are very good that he will act up on the way home. Allow him a loose rein and let him walk at his own speed as long as he stays at a walk. Keep your hands in a position that allow you to take up rein contact quickly in an emergency. Immediately bring him back to the walk if he breaks into a trot. Just as in the arena, when he returns to the

 When you offer your horse choices, you set him up for success by making the correct thing to do easier and more pleasant than the alternative.

desired speed reward him instantly with a loose rein and a lot of praise. You want to make his ride as pleasurable as possible. If he breaks into a trot and is reluctant to return to a walk, try taking him into a small circle—that will take the fun out of trotting. Occasionally a horse gets aggravated with this technique and when you finish your circle, he will dash forward instead of being happy to walk. You will have to experiment with your horse to find out the best way to cope with the problem.

If he is really fighting you on the way home, it is best just to get off and lead him. After a bad trip like that, you should work him at the barn after you get back so that rushing home to his stall does not become a reward for him. Working when he gets home, even for a few minutes, denies the horse positive reinforcement for his unacceptable behavior.

As soon as your horse is reliable at a walk and your confidence in him is high, it is time to introduce the trot. All the rules that apply to a walk apply to the trot with one additional rule: In the beginning, avoid trotting towards home unless you are a long distance away. If your horse has a serious runaway mentality, you should always walk the last half-hour and not take any chances. The last leg of the trail on the way home is his most vulnerable time, and is when you should be the most cautious.

At the trot, ride with either a loose rein or light contact as you did with the walk. Avoid a tight rein and a collected frame. Give him the freedom to work with long, loose strides and enjoy himself. One reason a horse wants to run away is because he wants to stretch his legs and move rather than be tightly controlled and collected. It is simply a form of rebellion. By letting him move out freely at the gait you choose rather than the gait he chooses, you come to a good compromise. If he is happy and comfortable, there is nothing for him to rebel against or escape from. He will sometimes accelerate and feel like he is going to break into a canter. The most effective thing to do then is to sit back and alternately pull on the reins. (Squeeze the left, release, squeeze the right, release…) It is tempting to keep a strong and steady contact, but this will give your horse something to brace against and actually may cause him to break into the canter.

You will know it is time to canter when your horse behaves well and your intuition tells you he is ready. Your friends with their well-behaved mounts may pressure you, but do not give in. Only you will know the right time, so don't follow the encouragement of others. Do not rush into the canter if you have any apprehensions at all. It could be days, weeks or even months, because every horse-human partnership is different, and there is no way an outsider can tell what is going on inside you and your horse. Take as long as necessary—there's nothing wrong with being cautious. When the time is right, you will feel it.

The day has come when you are ready to try the canter with your horse. To make the ride as successful as possible, take the precaution of stacking all the cards in your favor.

Request the canter in your typical manner and go only a short distance at first. Treat your horse the same way that you did at the walk and a trot. If all goes well—and it should—gradually add more and more cantering to your rides. Always praise him profusely for good behavior. Eventually you will be able to canter towards home. Go about it the same way as you did when you first started to canter away from home. If you don't feel safe in doing this, don't risk it. Nothing's wrong with doing a lot of trotting.

Sometimes carelessness or a lack of common sense causes a runaway situa-

Your intuition will tell you when the time is right to start cantering your runaway down trail. Ellen knows that she can handle Ranger at a canter here, even though the trail follows alongside a large open field.

Suggestions for a Successful First Canter on the Former Runaway

- Make sure he has trotted quite a bit and the edge is definitely taken off him.
- Choose to canter in the direction away from home.
- If you are riding with someone, have them ride a far distance behind you to be your "anchor." If they can go at a fast trot instead of a canter, that is even better. Galloping hooves close behind will encourage your horse to race.
- To help control his speed, try to find a long, up-sloping hill that is not too steep. Too steep a grade may make him excited. For some reason, horses like to go very fast up steep hills.

tion. My friend, who owns the Arabian mare that used to run away in arenas, went out on one of her first trail rides alone. She picked a bad day to ride because she was in the midst of a serious bout of the flu and was on very strong

No matter how well the confirmed runaway behaves, he is never totally cured, so always ride with a certain amount of caution. Here are some things to keep in mind:

- Never race him with other horses.
- Be careful in large groups where he might get excited.
- Avoid letting him gallop full-out.
- Always have a plan in the back of your mind for what to do if he gets a notion to run.
- Don't urge him to go faster in unfamiliar areas, for the excitement alone may cause him to bolt.
- Never, never go faster than a walk when you are within sight of home.

When the lead horse is cantering, the horse behind will naturally want to canter also. A horse that has a tendency to race may want to pass the leader. Photo © Linda Sherrill.

medication. Needless to say, her judgment was impaired. She rode several miles at a walk and her horse was doing superbly. She was so pleased that she thought she could try a canter (she had never cantered this horse on trail before). She should have tried to trot her horse on the trail before attempting to canter, but the real mistake was that she had already turned towards the barn when she started to canter. That was all the mare needed. She took off at the speed of light and didn't stop until my friend fell off. Fortunately, the horse did not leave her stranded in the park.

This same friend redeemed herself by showing excellent judgment about a month later when she was riding with a large group of people who were on their way to be in a parade. They got to a wide-open area that was only about a quarter mile long, ending at a road intersection. Since they were a little late, they wanted to canter that stretch of trail to make up time. My friend was uneasy with the situation since she had never cantered her horse with other horses. She asked the other riders not to canter, but they wouldn't relent. She turned back home because she wisely preferred missing the parade rather than risking a disaster if she couldn't stop her horse by the time they reached the road.

You must always think ahead when riding a horse that is prone to running away.

Never assume that your horse has mastered his bad habit; wait until he has proven that to you by behaving correctly in many different situations.

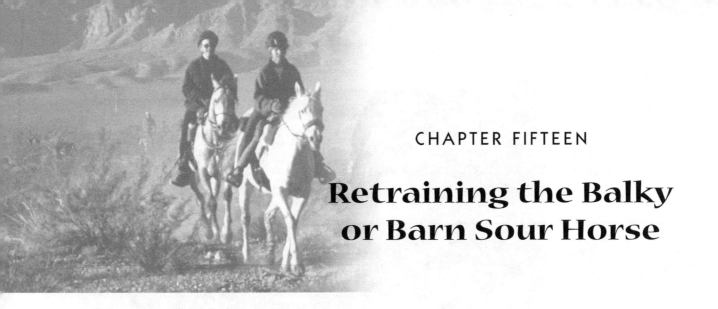

CHAPTER FIFTEEN

Retraining the Balky or Barn Sour Horse

Balking is a common habit that manifests itself in varying degrees ranging from a minor annoyance to a horse that won't leave the barn without a huge fight. It boils down to an unwillingness to go forward (usually away from home) and can also be called barn sour or herd bound. Often, the horses that are so reluctant to go out on the ride are more than happy to return to the barn. They just want to be with the safety of the herd and in the comfort of their home. Some horses that will back twenty or thirty steps rather than take one step forward away from home. Not being able to get out of the driveway is a great way to ruin a trail ride.

CAUSES OF BALKINESS

There are different causes of balkiness, so it is wise to diagnose the reason for your horse's behavior before you decide upon a remedy.

Your horse may be insecure and fearful of leaving the safety of his herd. Often these horses are fine if they have a companion; they only misbehave if they are ridden alone. One nine-year-old mare had been away from her original home just a couple of times in her life and never out on trail before. The

first time out she became so frightened on trail, even when ridden with other horses, that she acted completely irrationally and blocked out all communication, as though no one were riding her at all. The world simply terrified her, since all she'd known before was one barn and one pasture. Fear was definitely the cause of her behavior. As the fear went away and she began to trust her new owner, she started to relax on the trail and quit balking.

Bad riding can easily cause balkiness. If a rider is insecure and has too strong a bit and/or a heavy hand, she may actually be telling her horse to stop when she wants to tell him to go. The result is a confused horse, one that might just plant his feet and refuse to budge. Even worse, conflicting signals may lead to rearing. I've seen riders kicking their horse to go forward while unwittingly also pulling at their mouths. What message is the horse supposed to get here?

Riding with a bad seat or badly fitting saddle may cause pain in your horse's back and discourage forward movement. Some horses expect pain whenever they are ridden. It's no wonder they don't want to go out on trail.

If your horse is balky, honestly examine your riding. You may be unintentionally

133

It is okay to let your horse stop and look at an obstacle before asking him proceed. Photo © Joe Andrews.

My aunt rents out horses for guided trail rides. One year she bought a small black horse of unknown breeding to use as a rental. I rode the mare in the spring and was delighted with her eager attitude and ground-covering trot. She couldn't have been more than fourteen hands, but she kept up with the big horses and liked to be in the lead. The next time I rode her was six months later, and I was shocked at the difference. She was hard to get out of the driveway and went into several backing up fits even though she was following other horses. She just couldn't take the abuse of so many novice riders. In the fall, she had to be sold because she became downright dangerous. Most horses this stable uses just seem to accept whatever riders they get, but this mare was of a sensitive nature and naturally rebelled. Sensitive horses need sensitive riding.

causing the problem by sending conflicting messages to your horse or inflicting pain. At the minimum, poor riding contributes to the problem of balkiness, and at the maximum, it causes it. Most people believe they are riding well, but without outside help there is no way for them to know if this is, in actuality, true. Ignorance is bliss only for you, not your horse. Any horse that gets sore and does not enjoy himself on the ride will become unenthusiastic.

At one time, I shared a mare with someone else, and she always seemed to get sore after the other rider worked her. One day, I rode her when she was very sore from being ridden the day before, and she acted like a completely different horse from what I was used to. The ride ended with the mare dashing straight into a companion's horse and throwing me right into the other horse's legs. The incident really showed me how soreness can affect a horse's personality.

If you aren't currently taking lessons and don't have a competent instructor to give you advice, have a friend take some pictures or videotape your riding. Compare these pictures with the ones you find in a good book about riding and see how you stack up. If there is a big difference, part of your horse's balking problem could be you. Don't let the results discourage you, though—just view it as the starting point of a journey. Time spent improving your riding should help your horse's attitude and is certainly never a waste of time.

Also be sure to check your tack. Any ill-fitting tack will contribute to the problem. Make sure nothing is rubbing wrong or pinching your horse. This includes the bridle, the bit, any martingales or breast collars, and the girth. The saddle should be neither too narrow nor too wide. The saddle pad or blanket should be clean and smooth.

One last thing to be aware of is your horse's condition. A horse can become sour if he is worked harder than is comfortable for him. In other words, your first spring ride should not be three hours of cantering. I've seen a good number of people take their horses out after several months off and expect their horses to be able to do just what they did the summer before. If there is one thing a horse learns well, it's to avoid pain. Start your horse slowly if he hasn't been ridden for a few months.

A young or green horse that was previously willing may balk to test you and see what he can get away with. In fact, most horses will try this once or twice. The key is to stop the behavior right away, thereby preventing a bad habit from forming. The moment the horse stops, either boot him or tap him with a whip immediately and decisively

I had taken a Quarter Horse, Elizabeth, trail riding several times in the company of other horses and at least six times alone. One day assistance was needed to lead a group ride. I saw no reason why Elizabeth couldn't begin to earn her keep, so I said I'd ride lead. Even though she was with other horses, five minutes from the barn she said she refused to take one step further. I was forceful with my legs, yet all she did was bounce around and grunt fiercely. The simple solution was to have my fellow riders pass me up and take the lead. Unfortunately, the two riders I was with were afraid to do that, so we had to go back to the barn, and someone else took out the group. Elizabeth and I went right back out on the trail alone to tackle the problem. If I had left her at the barn, she would have learned she could get away with balking and get out of work.

Not surprisingly, Elizabeth balked at the exact same spot on the trail, but this time I was ready. I kept her going forward with my legs, never letting her to come to a complete stop. She continued hesitantly, and I felt I might have more problems ahead of me when a miracle happened. Someone else came by on horseback, and we rode the rest of the way together. I never had a serious problem with her from that day on. The most she ever did was pause, but a firm boot would easily get her going again.

to show him unequivocally that it is unacceptable behavior. As soon as your horse moves forward, give him a lot of praise. Hopefully, that is all that will be needed. If he won't go forward, but you can still get him to move, ask him to go sideways or in tiny circles. It is far more pleasant for your horse to move straight ahead, so you are making that option look very appealing to him, and the choice will be much easier.

A green horse that persists in giving you problems with balkiness is telling you he needs more work at home. Place your emphasis on obedience to go forward at all gaits in any direction you ask. If he is still good at trail riding when he is with other horses, continue riding with company to encourage good behavior and to prevent him from getting bored with ring work.

ARENA TRAINING

The work in the ring should be focused on solving the causes of the horse's reluctance to go forward. I recommend doing many figures and transitions. This horse is the opposite of the runaway that needs to learn to obey commands to slow down and stop. Here, your work should emphasize quick response to upward transitions. Be sure to spend some time backing up. Although you are not

To use a leading rein, bring your hand way out to the side to bend your horse's neck as Ellen is with Mingo.

going forward, you are still teaching the horse to move in the direction that you ask.

The time spent in the ring will also help to build your horse's confidence in you and change his opinion of you from an adversary to a herd member he can trust. Leaving the herd won't be so scary for him if he feels like he's bringing part of it with him.

TRAIL TRAINING

Don't try to go out on the trail alone until you are fully confident that your horse is thoroughly obedient in the arena to the basic commands and the concept of going forward. This way, the odds are in your favor, and you are setting the stage for success. There is a very good chance that if you are alone, a balky horse may try to balk. Here are some ideas on how to foil him.

At the first sign of refusal, glance around quickly to insure the horse is not afraid of something. Make sure he is just unwilling to go on. Immediate action on your part is vital. A good kick or smack with the whip may be enough, but if he is adamant, it may take more.

The approach to the problem will always hinge on the terrain. The terrain makes solutions more difficult on trail than in the arena. If there is enough room to maneuver in and the footing is safe, any of these options may work.

Try walk your horse into three to four small circles with a leading rein. At the end of these, right before you start to face the direction you want to go, boot him decisively down the path. The circling will distract him and change what he is thinking about. One of the joys of horse training is that most horses can think of only one thing at a time. By the time you boot him forward, he

Circle your balky horse a few times and give him a kick when he is facing the correct direction to drive him forward. Kevin has found this is extremely effective with RB.

may have forgotten why he was balking. At the same time, the circles serve as a consequence of the bad behavior. No horse likes to spin around in small circles, and it may deter him from balking again. Yet circling isn't excessively uncomfortable or inhumane. It is certainly better than spurs in his belly. If the spinning works, continue on in the right direction and waste no time in praising him and scratching his neck or withers.

Sometimes there isn't enough room to circle your horse on the trail. In that case, you can try a maneuver called *doubling*. Turn him 180 degrees in a very sharp bend, so he is facing towards home. Since this is the way he wants to go, he will turn with enthusiasm, and you will have created the necessary forward motion. You can do this at a walk or a trot. After he takes a couple steps, use the opposite hand with a leading

rein and turn him 180 degrees back in the original direction. As he comes out of the turn, aggressively drive him forward at a trot. Prepare yourself for some hesitation at the spot where he initially balked, and drive him through it. Once you have passed it, give him praise and more praise.

While you are doing this, don't keep a tight hold of the reins because it will send conflicting messages, and he may react by stepping sideways, backwards or rearing. Also, a looser rein will act as a reward.

Both of these methods are particularly useful if this is the type of horse that tries to turn home when he balks. Either keep spinning him or double him to get him going in the direction you want to travel. He will learn that turning towards home on his own is fruitless. You just have to keep on your toes, so that you can catch him as soon as he begins his turn.

Some horses will plant their feet into the ground and just refuse to budge. Try pulling this horse's head from side to side with a leading rein to shift his balance and force him to take a step to regain it. You can also get off and lead him. Even then, it still may be necessary to bend his head way to the side, or to turn his head from one side to the other several times, to get him to take a step. If that doesn't work, lift his foreleg and put it down to break the "freeze" in his mind. Another tactic is to do turns on the hindquarters or turns on the forequarters. Use anything that will get the horse moving and obeying your commands again. Encouraging him to lower his head to withers height will help him relax and become more cooperative.

Some people have success with just staying on a "frozen" horse until he gets bored or forgets the problem and moves

Bend the balky horse's head to the side and hold it there for a minute or two before asking him to move on.

When just a three-year-old colt, Mingo would freeze very badly when I first started to take him on short trail rides on his own. The odd thing about it was he would freeze after we turned back toward the barn. I really don't know what his motive for balking was, other than the need for more basic training. Absolutely nothing would work to get him to take a step except another horse coming by that he could follow. Finally I started to pull his head to the side and keep it there for a couple minutes. It took no time at all for him to learn that balking on the trail is unacceptable. Now, if he balks, I simply pull his head out to the side for twenty seconds and he is happy to continue on our way when I straighten him out.

on his own. That is when you praise him profusely. This requires a lot of time and patience on the part of the rider. It would possibly work better if you have a friend come by on horseback ten to fifteen minutes later so your horse will have a good incentive and reward for moving off in the right way. This may have to be done numerous times to create a new mindset.

Another spin on the "wait it out" method is to bring his head out to the side with your rein and hold it there for several minutes. This is an uncomfortable position for the horse since he is off-balance, and so the waiting time will be decreased. Eventually, he will want to take a step forward to regain his balance. That is when you release the rein and praise him. If you are standing for a long time like this, perhaps he hasn't figured out that he will feel better by going forward. Release the rein and ask him to step forward. If this doesn't work, pull his head out to the side again and wait a while longer. Eventually, he will see the light.

The average horse will repeatedly balk at the same spots each time, particularly if he was successful at any time in the past. Your job is to anticipate the problem and have a plan ready. If you can trot through the area when you near the spot, the forward momentum and encouragement with your legs may keep him going on through it. He may drop to a walk, but at least that still gives you a chance to keep him from stopping completely. Be firm and quiet, and always praise for even the tiniest amount of cooperation.

In general, balky horses must be ridden with a lot of awareness. No day dreaming is allowed. Always be alert for an unasked shortening of stride. Driving the horse forward with your legs can stop a problem before it starts, or at least

Kevin is using leading reins on both sides of RB so that he can only go forward.

can prevent the balk from becoming worse than a slight pause.

On occasion, you will meet up with a horse that is so balky he goes into reverse. If you are lucky, you will be in a spot that you can maneuver him into something uncomfortable like thorny bushes. I've never been that lucky. But I have had good success in stopping this behavior by first leaning extremely far back in the saddle to throw my weight on the horse's hindquarters and impede his motion, and then giving a firm and decisive kick. At the same time, make sure your reins are not telling him to back. A loose rein will allow him to shift into forward motion.

Your horse may be the kind that is very anxious to get home and is hard to control as soon as you are headed back to the barn. This is when the balky horse turns into a prancer or jogger. Some horses will act better if they are led rather than ridden when first turned to face home. In this case, lead for a while as you start home, and then when your horse settles down, mount up again, and he may retain his quiet mood.

It's always best to do your fast work when traveling away from the barn. It will tire the horse and help him to be quieter on the return trip. If he is at all excited from doing the faster work, walk for a while to calm him down before you turn around, so that he will be quieter for the ride home. Lots of praise and a loose rein will encourage his good behavior. You may even want to train him to walk on a loose rein as I described in retraining the runaway horse.

Occasionally, as you approach the stable or trailer, it is a good idea to pass up any type of trail leading directly there. This will teach your horse that you decide when to go home and that just because you are going in that direction, it doesn't mean you will go back to the barn and unsaddle. There may be times when you really do want to pass up the barn. This lesson is good for all horses, not just those horses that are barn sour.

Lastly, if your horse is really difficult on the way back, don't put him directly into his stall or pasture. This is just what he wants, and it will function as a reward. Rather, do some arena work so that he doesn't have a reason to hurry home next time.

CHAPTER SIXTEEN

Retraining the Horse that Prances or Rears

Prancing and rearing have similar causes, and a horse that prances may take up rearing if the cause of his prancing is not removed. These horses want to go somewhere, but they can't. They take the energy of their forward movement and direct it upwards. Eventually, they may go straight up.

PRANCING

One of the most annoying habits and a very difficult (but not impossible) one to break is jogging or prancing (jibbing). These horses are typically the worst on the way home because they are in a hurry to get to the barn.

I used to ride with a Quarter Horse mare that would not willingly walk a single step. She could jog all day and not go any faster than my horse walking right beside her. Since the impact of the trot is greater on the joints than the impact of the walk, it could have been harmful to the mare. This mare was generally held back with a short rein to keep her slow and wasn't allowed to move with a long, loose stride. She was always in a cramped frame (not the rounded, lovely frame of a well-trained horse that is asked for in correct collection). The mare's ears would

always be slightly pinned to her head, her eyes squinted, her chin and lips tight, and she would have a pained look on her face. She ended up being retired at only twenty years of age due to lameness and a very sore back. It's likely that the years of jogging in a slow, cramped position instead of walking comfortably took their toll. Let me be clear: I'm not disparaging the slow western jog on a loose rein that many horses are trained to do. It's the "hold the reins tight to keep him from taking off" gait that I refer to here.

Your retraining program will depend on how badly your horse behaves. A horse with a mild problem will start to prance or jog as a way of asking the rider to go faster. Even if you had intended to increase your gait, you must change your plan and stay at a walk to prevent a minor problem from escalating. Tell your horse "no" by pulling and releasing the reins until he walks. To reward him, allow him to walk on a loose rein and praise him. He may try to jog again as soon as you give him the loose rein, but patiently keep up the process until he understands. After he has been going along well for a while and seems calm, then you can ask him to increase his speed. He needs to learn that you are the one who decides at what speed to travel. Why

Simply pulling the reins back when your horse tries to prance will not slow him down. It is just giving RB something to fight against.

should you be so fussy? Simply because this problem can become very serious in no time at all, and it is such a difficult habit to change.

My sister's horse, Ranger, had a mild case of jogging. Through trial and error, she discovered that if she immediately released the reins when he walked, he nearly always went back into the jog. On the other hand, if she held the reins for a couple of strides of the walk and then released them, he'd be fine. This goes against the theory of immediate reward, but not everything works exactly the way the books say it should. You may have to experiment to find what works the best for your horse.

A more persistent jogger requires a more aggressive plan of action. It is helpful to ride with a companion whose horse will remain at a walk regardless of what other horses in the group are doing. Such a horse will set a good example and may work as an anchor to keep you from jogging ahead, because

he won't want to leave his friend behind.

Your objective is to teach your mount to relax, lower his head and enjoy a loose-reined walk. A loose rein is essential because a jogger or prancer likes to have something to push against. Prancers, in particular, seem to relish it.

The first thing to do is to set the stage so that your horse wants to walk. In other words, get him tired! Don't take him out and expect him to walk when he is loaded with excess energy and really wanting to go. Most horses jog the most when they are going towards home. In fact, many horses only jog on the way home. To get the horse tired, work him really hard on the way out so that when you turn towards home, he sighs and says, "Oh good, I'm tired and I want to walk. I'm glad my rider is letting me." Most likely, he won't think of that immediately, but if he is tired, it will be easier to convince him.

A friend, Pete, once leased a Tennessee Walker mare whose owners no longer had time to ride. The little black mare was quiet, patient and unflappable—that is until a rider got on her back. She then transformed into unstoppable. She wanted to do her gait, and she wanted to do it fast.

Her age was something over twenty, so this habit was deeply ingrained. Her owners simply kept using more and more severe bits. The last one looked like a medieval torture device. It was some sort of long-shanked, double-twisted wire contraption. She gaited right through that one, too. It seemed hopeless.

The mare would get back to the barn so sweaty that it took half an hour to cool her off. Pete worked with her for a few weeks before she would walk quietly, and ended up riding her with a fairly mild curb. When he brought her back to the barn, she was quiet and relaxed—not sweaty and wound up. The last time I spoke with Pete, he let me know that his horse was walking quietly in a snaffle bit. I'm sure they will have many miles of happy trails ahead of them.

As you are going away from the barn, insist that the horse moves at an energetic trot. Avoid the western jog. He can probably do that all day without tiring. Western riders may want to learn to post if they don't already know. It isn't too difficult to post in a western saddle, and it will encourage your horse to keep his speed up. Also, be very firm about which gait you want. Allowing a horse to break into a canter when you are trotting isn't much different from going from a walk to a jog. The discipline will help you when you are combating the jog.

Sometimes circumstances don't permit you to work your horse really hard on trail. Some riders have many miles of trail available, but few places where they can travel faster than a slow trot. In that situation, try to get your horse tired before you head out on trail by longeing him or riding in an arena.

Horses that strain against tight reins are not comfortable, but they are doing the only thing they know. If they don't like the rein, they either pull harder at the bit, which hurts their mouth, or they back off the bit, which cramps their neck. A thoughtful rider wants to teach her horse to seek the relief of the loose rein. It is natural for a rider to keep pulling harder to slow down her prancing horse, but what she really needs to do is to learn to let go.

I suggest working your horse to the point where he wants to take a break. At that time, ask him to walk. As soon as he does, let the reins go slack. If possible, let them become very long so they flop all around as he walks. If he won't walk at all, just reward him with a slack rein for slowing down, and use that as your starting point.

If he is unaccustomed to loose reins the horse may dash forward upon release

Some horses that are trained to walk on the loose rein will figure out that you want to pick up the speed when you pick up the reins. As long as you are firm with them and don't allow them to move out until the proper cue is given, you will get a nice side effect. By picking up the reins, you warn your horse of a gait change, and you get his attention. He will begin to prepare for a transition. Then, when you ask for the gait change, he will move out promptly.

Asking a crowding horse to stop and back a few steps is another way of teaching him not to prance and jog.

of the reins. Many horses do. This is the part of the training that calls for patience. Quickly pick the reins up, take the slack out of them and ask him to walk again. You will have to keep doing this until he will walk quietly on a loose rein. As he improves, keep giving him more and more rein and a lot of verbal praise. Rub his neck and scratch his withers, too—do anything that conveys to him how happy you are with what he is doing. Walk him for the rest of your ride and then give him the ultimate reward—quit for the day. Keep working on this lesson until he will quietly walk with a loose rein. Soon he will begin looking for it.

When you are heading towards home, the really persistent prancer may have to be turned around, booted into a brisk trot for twenty feet or so, turned back and asked to walk. Keep repeating this lesson until he decides to walk. I've heard this referred to as "taking the long way home." Hopefully, it won't be long before he sees that he is going nowhere and decides to be more cooperative.

The problem of prancing definitely won't be solved overnight, and it will most likely take weeks of patience before you get any major improvement. Results will come much faster if you work consistently rather than letting your horse get away with prancing every now and then.

The worst kind of prancer or jogger is the one that doesn't have a clue as to what you want. It's possible that a previous owner let him do whatever he wanted and so he learned no discipline. He may be jogging because he is so nervous or excited that he is unable to listen to you. In either case, this horse is not ready for trail riding. Instead, go back to basics in the arena and completely retrain him. It might be awhile before you can get back on trail, but at least when you do, you'll be able to enjoy yourself.

REARING

If your horse rears regardless of where you ride him, don't try to solve the problem on the trail. This kind of horse should not be out on trail until he is completely safe at home. Work with him in as safe an arena as you can find, and don't venture back out on the trail until he has vastly improved. If the problem is really serious and you can't cope with it, either seek a professional trainer or sell the horse. Safety is always of paramount importance.

Rearing horses typically are not born, but created. A horse usually rears because there is a reason, and very often, the reason is the rider and/or a bit that is too severe.

A horse that is prone to rear will often prance or jog, keeping his mouth behind the bit. Rearing can be caused by the same thing as prancing—heavy hands and conflicting signals. A rider who hangs onto the reins too tightly and still asks the horse to go forward is telling the horse to move, but is not letting him, so the horse has nowhere to go but up. The rider then must loosen the reins to prevent her mount from going over backwards, and the horse is rewarded by the cessation of pain in his mouth. Even better, from the horse's point of view, is when the rider falls off or gets scared and turns back home. Once again, he is rewarded. (The Lippizans are taught the levade in the manner described above, except they are taught gently and gradually so that the result is a beautiful, controlled movement rather than a terrifying one.)

If a horse has never reared before and suddenly begins the habit while you are riding, ask yourself if you are nervous and unknowingly holding too tightly onto the reins. Some people are fine in the arena, but tense up as soon as they get out on the trail. This kind of rider needs to make a conscious effort to loosen up the reins, sit back and relax. Riding lessons can help you significantly by improving your skills, balance and raising your confidence level.

If your horse rears, you must always be very aware of how you are riding. Your hands should only have a light contact on the bit, always giving the horse the choice of moving forward instead of up. When asking the horse to stop or slow down, you should immediately relinquish the reins as soon as the horse responds. If the horse tries to speed up again, slow him down by pulling and releasing repetitively until the desired results are achieved. Always avoid strong, constant contact.

Ride forward with a lot of impulsion and energy. This is not the time to work on the jog-trot or any collected gaits. Just allowing your horse to move in a free-flowing walk or extended trot, if he's not accustomed to it, may help the problem considerably. Keep in mind that rearing is caused by the channeling of energy upward instead of forward. Your aim is to reverse the process by changing the direction of impulsion.

You must diligently monitor the horse's movements. If his energy is flowing forward, in order to rear he will have to pause to switch that energy upward. It's much the same as if you were running and decided to hop in one spot: You would have to pause between the movements. As soon as you feel your horse make that pause, do everything in your power to convince him he'd rather continue forward. Take extra care not to pull back on the reins, which would only encourage him to rear. A rider who is very attentive may notice a slight lightness in the front of the horse when he is just thinking about rearing. A good boot in the ribs at that moment may be all that is needed to get your horse moving forward again.

When determining the cause of rearing, the next place to look is the bit. I've noticed that, for some reason, most rearers wear a curb bit. Although a curb bit is often necessary with horses that are difficult to stop or slow down, it can do more harm than good with a horse that rears and a rider who lacks the finesse to use a curb bit well. These bits are not meant for a strong, constant contact; rather, there should be some slack in the reins, and the horse should be primarily neck reined. Unless your horse is bad about slowing and stopping, a snaffle bit is far more appropriate for a rearing horse. The two of you should spend quite a lot of time in the arena when you

first switch to a snaffle bit to get used to the way the bit works.

Another thing to check is the fit of the bit. It should be neither too large, with a lot of play from side to side, nor so small that it pinches. Inspect it for any sharp edges that may cut the horse's tongue or cheeks. The bit should be adjusted so it isn't too low or high in the mouth. A bit that's too low will bang the horse's teeth, and a bit that's too high will pinch the corners of his mouth. While you are at it, check that the curb chain isn't too tight and that it lies flat against his chin. It's surprising the number of twisted curb chains I've seen on horses.

There will be times, particularly in the beginning of his retraining, that your horse will be one step ahead of you and will succeed in rearing. Be prepared. You should have a well-rehearsed plan in your mind as to how you will respond when he does rear. This way, even if fear causes your thinking process to become

This is the position to get into when your horse rears. Photo by Ellen Daly.

confused or freeze up, you will know what to do. Mentally rehearse your plan until you are sure you can do it even in a moment when you might otherwise panic.

As your horse goes up into the air, lean forward and move your hands toward the bit. A rider leaning back and pulling the reins is the main cause of horses falling over backwards, and that's the last thing you want! Shifting your weight forward will put weight on your horse's forehand and discourage him from rearing too high. Practice going into your rearing position when your horse is at a standstill. You must be able to do this without hesitation whenever the situation arises.

A horse can't remain in a rearing position forever; he has to come back down. As his feet are just about to touch the ground, explosively drive him forward. Put one hand close to the bit, low and out to the side, and force the horse to go in small circles. Better yet, if the trail conditions are right, spin him in a half circle one way and then spin him in another half circle in the opposite way. As you are about to finish, boot him forward in the direction you want to go and don't let him slow or stop until you are ready.

This maneuver is another reason to avoid a curb bit—if done with a curb, it can cause a great deal of mouth pain. The best snaffle for the job is a full cheek or a D-ring because these can't be pulled through the horse's mouth and the long sides encourage the horse to laterally bend his neck. Since a horse must stop in order to repeat this behavior, do not to allow him to stop of his own volition after a rear. As soon as you get a chance, however, check to determine that the saddle is still in position and hasn't slipped backwards.

A horse that likes to rear may not be very good at standing as you talk to

Upon landing from a rear, promptly bring your horse into sharp circles as a reprimand. Photo © John Burkett.

You will probably hear many "cures" for your horse offered by people trying to be helpful. Before you attempt any of them, think the solution through very thoroughly. Some of the ways to stop a rearing horse that I've been told are fairly bizarre; for example, hitting him on top of the head with a two-liter bottle filled with water that will break and dump water on the horse, or sliding off his back and pulling him to the ground. Even if they worked, the potential for injury is great. The methods offered here are safe, humane and lean mostly towards preventing the incidents from happening in the first place.

other people while you are mounted. Trying to hold an anxious horse in one position can easily cause him to rear. Ask friends to ride with you while you talk, and explain the situation to them. Any reasonable person will certainly understand. You can work on the problem a little at a time in the arena. Stop your horse after a good hard workout and ask him to stand for a short time without dismounting. Gradually increase the time as he becomes more relaxed. Praise him lavishly for standing quietly and reward him by either dismounting and quitting for the day or taking a quick jog around the arena. If at first your horse refuses to stand at all when you are mounted, work on standing him in the arena with other horses for short intervals while you are on the ground and leading him. With time and patience, he should learn this lesson. It's really not safe to take him on the trail until he has learned it well.

CHAPTER SEVENTEEN

Retraining the Horse that Bucks or Spooks

BUCKING

It is not unusual for a horse to buck now and then due to high spirits or excitement, particularly if he is young or has been cooped up for a while. Bucking on a regular basis, though, should not be ignored. Bucking is an especially bad habit for a trail horse because if you get bucked off, it may be a long walk home. Even worse, if you are hurt, it can escalate into an emergency situation when help is hard to find.

In the case of a horse that bucks from being confined in the barn too much, just increasing his exercise will alleviate most of the problem. Turn him out more often. Even a couple of times a week can make a big difference, and it works best if he is with a companion that will run and play with him. Mingo just loves to buck whenever he has an excuse. By letting him buck while he's turned out to play, he gets it out of his system and will not buck when I ride him. On the cold days that I don't have time to turn him out first, I end up paying for my mistake. Usually, the first fifteen or twenty minutes can be tricky, and I must be on guard for his playful behavior. Bucking under saddle is his way of telling me that all work and no

play makes a rambunctious horse. Once I get him trotting for a bit, however, he will start to settle down, and I can then enjoy my ride.

Depending on your situation, it may be hard to turn your horse out. I've been at boarding stables where an empty ring is a rare occurrence. Some places won't let you turn your horse loose in the riding area. Even in the places that do, you are at the mercy of inclement weather and bad footing conditions. Sometimes a horse that is turned loose just stands and looks at you or grazes—this won't do too much good. It may be necessary to longe this horse, or ride him in the arena to take the edge off. The solution may be that you need to ride one or two times more each week, find someone else to share the responsibility of riding, take your horse on longer or more vigorous rides, or reduce his feed. Whatever you do, don't cut back on riding because you are afraid of him bucking—that will only make him worse. If you are frightened, longe him before riding to insure the worst of his antics are over before you get in the saddle. Every buck on a longe line is one less buck that you will have to ride.

A horse that is a serious bucker should not be taken on trail until he behaves well at home. Sometimes seeking

You may need to work your horse in the arena to take the edge off him before you go out on the trail.

Sue is doubling Angel to the right to get control of her and reprimand her for bucking. After doing a 180-degree turn to the right, she will do the same to the left. Photo by Erin Smith.

professional help from a reputable trainer is the best thing you can do. Swallow your pride and ask for help if you need it. Being bucked off on trail with your horse galloping riderless towards home is not only dangerous, it's a great way to reinforce a bad habit.

As your horse starts to buck, bring his head up by pulling upward, not back, with the reins. At the same time, lean your body back and brace your arms against your sides so he can't pull the reins out of your hands and get his head down. A horse that wants to buck high has to bring his head way down to the ground. Picture the classic bucking broncos with their heads low. To keep your horse from becoming a bucking bronco, drive him forward using whatever you can—your seat, legs or whip—and give him a firm vocal reprimand. If you have a whip, smack him on the shoulders, not the hindquarters (which would encourage him to buck more). At all costs, keep your horse moving forward. As in controlling rearing, it's a matter of channeling his energy forward instead of upward.

If your horse bucks a lot, whether in the ring or out on trail, catch him on the first buck and turn him sharply first one way and then the other to double him as described in the discussion on balking. After doubling him a few times, get him to move briskly forward. Horses just hate playing that doubling game.

A method that works well to halt Mingo's playful bucking is making him spin three to four times in a row in the same direction. He is mostly Quarter Horse and has a terrific spin, but that doesn't mean he likes to do it. I pull his head to the right and smack his hindquarters on the same side with the whip. (I'm right-handed, so it is my stronger side.) This usually takes the wind out of his sails, and the game is no longer fun for him.

Most horses that buck because of excess energy will do it at the canter. It seems to be a natural movement. Even in play, that is when they buck most often. Doing a lot of fast trotting to tire your horse before you canter can counteract this. Also, try cantering uphill if your horse wants to buck. It is very strenuous to buck uphill and this will discourage him. Because it is hard for horses to buck high when they are going fast, you are actually safer at the faster speed.

To keep from being taken by surprise, learn your horse's particular actions that signal he is planning to buck. For example, he may lay his ears back or drop his head as a precursor to bucking. Cruiser seldom bucks, but when he does, he tries to pull the reins out of my hands like a dog playing tug-of-war. No one could miss that cue! Mingo will arch his neck, go behind the bit and grunt. Interestingly, his mother did the exact same thing when she wanted to buck. It is possible that merely keeping your horse's head up and giving him strong vocal reprimands when he gives you any of his signals will minimize or even eliminate his urge to buck. If I think a horse is going to buck, I also boot him strongly with my legs to keep him moving briskly forward. Forward is better than upward!

If your normally quiet horse bucks, he may be reacting to discomfort. Check your tack and also look for sore spots on his withers, back and girth area. Continuing your ride may make matters worse. Something as simple as a crinkle in a saddle blanket can make horse's back very sore in just a few hours. To prevent this, before you mount for your ride, quickly do a safety check to make sure all your tack is in order. Make sure

By keeping his head up and kicking him forward, I am thwarting Mingo's effort to buck. Photo by Kevin Curry.

that your blanket or pad is clean and smooth. The only time Mingo ever succeeded in bucking someone off when saddle pad slipped back a few inches. Mingo was so disturbed by this that instead of doing his typical small, playful buck, he made three huge bucks.

SPOOKING

A spooky horse isn't necessarily a serious problem; it depends on the degree of spooking, your riding skill and your tolerance level.

The horse you are riding may be trotting along happily and suddenly give a little jump and then continue as if nothing even happened. Chances are good that he is only adjusting the position of his body so he can see an object from a different angle. As soon as things become clear, he dismisses the scary object from his mind

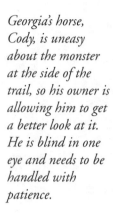

Georgia's horse, Cody, is uneasy about the monster at the side of the trail, so his owner is allowing him to get a better look at it. He is blind in one eye and needs to be handled with patience.

and resumes traveling. My sister's horse, Ranger, does this continually, and she just accepts it as the norm. She has learned to ride with a lot of awareness and a strong seat. The faster they go, the more likely that Ranger will shy and the stronger her seat must be. A horse whose eyes are set more to the side of his head than to the front, like Ranger, has less binocular vision and is more likely to shy in this manner. Ranger always shies more when he is feeling frisky, so my sister has learned to drive him forward when she sees signs of him being silly and wanting to shy at imaginary objects.

Although shying can be disconcerting, you should stay calm and dismiss the spooking as quickly as your horse dismisses them. This kind of spooking is usually harmless as long as you retain your seat. If you are caught by surprise and lose your balance, you are more likely to stay on board if you lean forward, even to the extent of grabbing the neck to avoid being left behind. Don't punish the horse in this situation, because it is

you who lost your balance, and punishment will make him think that there really was something to be afraid of.

Spooking, like bucking, is often related to the amount of exercise a horse is getting. A horse can easily get overexcited if he hasn't been worked in a while. Spooking is one vice that is guaranteed to decrease as riding increases. A lot of it is caused by the lack of exercise and the desire to play. Indeed, many horses will play "spook" when they are turned out in the pasture. It's a good idea to turn your horse out if he has been confined for a while and has the tendency to spook—that way, he can do his playing without you on his back.

A horse with a serious spooking problem is one that gets so frightened that he wants to turn and bolt home. A horse that absolutely refuses to pass an object on the trail is not dangerous, but he sure can ruin a ride. All horses have a few bad moments now and then, but if your horse has more than his share, go back to the section on training young horses and treat

At a barn where I used to board, there was an older, gentle horse whose owner wasn't interested in showing or working in the arena. She typically only visited her horse once a month. He got so fat and out of condition that she vowed to ride him at least every weekend. The first time they went out, he spooked constantly and frightened her. She tried the following weekend, with the same results. That was the last time she rode. If she had stuck to her plan it is fairly certain that the shying would have steadily decreased. Her horse had a very quiet nature and just hadn't been ridden in such a long time that he became overly energetic and excited that he was on trail. Combine this with the fact that the trails were new to him, and you have a great recipe for spooking.

Legend has it that Arabians were bred to be spooky because their Arab masters wanted horses that would scan the horizon and warn them of any approaching enemy. Looking at it in this light, it's not so bad to have a very alert horse that may shy every now and then. In some ways, it can aid in making a great trail horse. Cruiser, my Half Arab, will warn me of mountain bikers, loose dogs, deer or strange people long before I discover them. He is past the stage of trying to run away; rather, he points things out to me and allows me to use my judgment as to whether it is safe to go on or not. He warns me so far in advance, it gives me time to prepare not only myself but everyone else in my group for potential problems. As a colt, Cruiser spooked at nearly everything, but now he's a joy to ride. After long confinements due to weather or injury, however, he reverts to his old ways and becomes very volatile. I have learned to either turn him out, longe him or expect a very wild ride!

him just as you would a youngster on his first rides. Chances are good that this horse simply was not accustomed to trail riding at a young age. The best thing you can do for him is to start all over from the beginning. It will probably take longer to quiet him than a young horse, because the older a horse gets, the less open-minded he becomes. Once again, patience and persistence shall prevail.

Conclusion

Often as I talk about my horses to the non-horse people I meet on the trail, I make comments like, "He says the weather is too hot to do a lot of fast riding," or "He says there is something up ahead on the trail," or "He says he wants to visit the horse over there." The people I am speaking to have two reactions: Either they think I am making these things up or they are astonished that I can tell so easily what the horse is thinking.

Horses communicate mostly through body language, and anyone who is around them enough can't help but learn it. Some things are general knowledge, such as a horse is angry when he lays back his ears or is irritated when he swishes his tail. The language can also be very subtle and varies from horse to horse. Sometimes Cruiser will lay his ears back and he isn't angry in the least. If he does it with a happy face, it is a submissive gesture and means he wants a treat. Even experienced horsepeople can be fooled by that move. It is a wise horseperson who takes the time to learn the body language of horses in general and their own horse's idiosyncrasies in particular. Not only are we are safer when we know what our horses are thinking, but it also enhances the pleasure of horse ownership.

Since we also use our sense of feel as we ride, we have an advantage that other animal owners lack. We can feel our horse tense up when he is scared or hesitate when he plans to balk, and we know if he's feeling sore from yesterday's ride. Often, I can feel the amount of energy he has, even if he isn't using it at that moment. At these times, I know better than to go galloping off down the trail with another horse because it will soon turn into a race, possibly with some bucking thrown in for fun. As horse owners, our job is to awaken all our senses so we can understand our horses better.

Trail riding develops a closer relationship between horse and rider than almost any other horse sport. It may be the result of the amount of time spent together, the adventures shared or the trust that is necessary in a good trail partnership. Probably it is a little of each. Horse shows are stressful and distracting. Out on the trail, we are more relaxed, and we are open to deeper communication. It's just the rider, the horse and the trail. The bonds built are strong.

I also believe if we spend a lot of time riding and caring for a particular horse we become "psychically bonded." This has happened with every horse I've taken care of for more than six months, and it is a difficult thing to explain. Eventually I become able to feel the horse's emotions—I know if he is happy, depressed, distracted or content. I don't know whether this happens because I am so closely tuned in to their body language, picking up their signals subconsciously, or because we communicate on a telepathic level. I've observed horses turned loose in groups, and it often looks as though they can communicate without any visible or audible language. For example, at times they will all dart off simultaneously for no apparent reason. If they can communicate telepathically with other horses, there certainly isn't any reason they couldn't communicate telepathically with us if we are open-minded.

Just as easily as I read them, my horses seem to pick up on my own emotions. If I'm depressed, they try to cheer me up. On days that I feel irritable, they know not to push my patience, and when I'm really happy, they join in my happiness and we have a terrific day.

A special bond is formed on the trail. Photo © K. S. Swigart.

My most intense occurrence of possible telepathic communication may seem far-fetched, and I shared it with few people before I discovered that an almost identical thing occurred between a friend and his wife and their dog. My very first horse, Brandy, was a wonderful old timer. I owned him for over two years and during that time, we were nearly inseparable. At the age of twenty-four, he became very ill. There was some hope of his recovery, but the last day was so bad that I called the vet out to put him to sleep. The vet agreed with me and was ready to put him down when the owner of the stables, seeing my distress, said she would help the vet if I couldn't watch. I thanked her and got in my car and headed for home.

The misery and sadness I felt as I was driving down the street crying was the same as losing a close member of the family. I halted at a stop sign, and at that instant, I felt an incredibly strong sensation of the easing of pain. It came in a wave so sudden and intense that if I had been standing, I might have fallen. I truly believe that what I felt was the release of Brandy's suffering. It didn't keep me from missing my dear old friend, but at least I had the comfort of knowing he was better off, and that I made the right decision.

Was it just a coincidence that I misinterpreted, or was it really a feeling I shared with Brandy in his last moments? There is no way to prove it either way. I do know that we had a very close relationship which probably would never have developed had we not spent many hours out on the trail together.

I sincerely hope that everyone who reads this book will also form a bond of such strength with their horses. There is no better place to build a strong relationship with your horse than on the trail where good two-way communication and a solid partnership is almost a necessity. I wish you miles and miles of safe and happy trails.

About the Author

Judi Daly has been an avid trail rider for many years, and routinely rides more than 1,000 miles on trail each year. In 1998, she was ranked in the top ten trail mile holders statewide for the Ohio Horse Council. When Judi first started trail riding, she found out the hard way that it was more than just hopping on a horse and cantering off into the sunset. She began to search for information on training her horses for the trail, but found little of help. Determined to learn as much as she could in order to trail ride successfully, she developed a program to teach her horses to be dependable and happy mounts. Her journey involved both retraining problem horses and training green horses from scratch.

In 2000 Judi developed a website devoted to the subject. She has also published articles on this topic.

This book, which began as an e-book, is a cumulation of information acquired through Judi's research, practical experience, and what she has learned from other horse people on the same journey. It is her hope that others can be spared some of the struggles she experienced and be encouraged to share the joy of trail riding.

Bibliography

Bradbury, Peggy. *Horse Safety Handbook.* Houston: Cordovan Corporation, Publishers, 1977.

Brown, Kathleen. "Don't Sweat It," *Horseman Magazine* (May 1985).

Browning, Sinclair. "Proper Ponying Starts on a Well-Broke Horse," *Horseman Magazine* (June 1988).

Browning, Sinclair. "Traveling Light," *Horse Illustrated* (June 1990).

Caddell, Linda Blake. "Heat Stress," *Horseman Magazine* (June 1988).

Clary, Anna. "Sundown is Coming," *Horseman Magazine* (November 1988).

Crabbe, Barb. "Trail Terrors," *Horse & Rider* (May 1994).

Giffen M.D., James M. and Tom Gore, D.V.M. *Horse Owner's Veterinary Handbook.* New York: Howell Book House, Inc., 1989.

Hill, Cherry. *Becoming an Effective Rider.* Pownal, VT: Storey Communications, Inc., 1991.

Hill, Cherry. "First Aid Procedures for Equestrian Accidents," *Horseman Magazine* (August 1987).

Hill, Cherry. *Making Not Breaking—The First Year Under Saddle.* New York: Breakthrough Publications, 1992.

Hill, Cherry. "Open Roads," *Horseman Magazine* (September 1987).

Hill, Cherry. "Tips for Winter Riding," *Horse and Rider Magazine* (December 1990).

Hill, Cherry. "Trail Rider's First Aid Kit," *Horseman Magazine* (March 1987).

Holderness Roddam, Jane. *Fitness for the Horse and Rider.* London: David and Charles Publishers, 1993.

Jacobs, D. T. "Ten Pacing Tactics for Endurance Riding," *Horseman Magazine* (November 1985).

Kadash, Kathy. "Mountain So High, Valley So Low," *Horseman Magazine* (August 1989).

Lynch, Betsy. "When a Rider takes a Fall," *Horseman Magazine* (July 1985).

Lyons, John. *Lyons on Horses.* New York: Doubleday, 1991.

McBane, Susan. *Behavior Problems in Horses.* London: David and Charles Publishers, 1987.

McGill, Debra. "The Signs of Stress: Know Them," *Horseman Magazine* (September 1981).

Mizwah, Tad. "Coping with the Heat," *Horseman Magazine* (June 1979).

Moore, Leslie. "Staying Warm," *Horseman Magazine* (August 1989).

Rashid, Mark. *Considering the Horse.* Boulder: Johnson Books, 1993.

Rees, Lucy. *The Horse's Mind.* New York: Prentice Hall Press, 1985.

Self, Margaret Cabell. *Fun on Horseback.* New York: Arco Publishing Company, Inc., 1945.

Self, Margaret Cabell. *The Horseman's Companion.* New York: A. S. Barnes and Company, Inc., 1949.

Self, Margaret Cabell. *The Horseman's Encyclopedia.* New York: A. S. Barnes and Company, Inc., 1946.

Taveres, Nancy. "Shy," *Horseman Magazine* (January 1982).

Twelveponies, Mary. *Everyday Training: Backyard Dressage.* Millwood, New York: Breakthrough Publications, 1980.

Twelveponies, Mary. *Starting the Colt.* New York: The Stephen Greene Press/Pelham Books, 1990.

Twelveponies, Mary. *There Are No Problem Horses, Only Problem Riders.* Boston: Houghton Mifflin Company, 1982.

Vincent, Sharon Garver. "First Aid for Horseman," *Horseman Magazine* (February 1979).

Young, John Richard. *The Schooling of the Horse.* The University of Oklahoma Press, Norman Publishing Division of the University of Oklahoma, 1982.

The lead rider waits until the riders following have safely descended the hill. Photo © Kim Andrews.

Other Sources of Information

Magazines with Trail Riding Information

The Trail Rider Magazine
P.O. Box 5089
Alexandria, LA 71307
1-800-448-1154
www.trailridermagazine.com

Trail Blazer Magazine
For both trail and competitive trail/endurance riders.
4241 North Covina Circle
Prescott Valley, AZ 86314-5419

The Trailrider's Journal
This magazine is for the southeast USA
3400 Mesa Drive
Flower Mound, TX 75022-6305
www.thetrailridersjournal.com

Horse Illustrated
General interest with some trail riding articles.
3 Burroughs
Irvine, CA 92618
(949) 855-8822, Fax (949) 855-3045
www.animalnetwork.com/horse

Horse and Rider
General interest with some trail riding articles.
Primedia Equine Network
656 Quince Orchard Road – Suit 600
Gaithersburg, MD 20878
(301) 977-3900
store.primediamags.com/subscibe/horseandrider

Books

Clayton, Hilary M. *Conditioning Sport Horses.* Saskatoon, Saskatchewan: Sport Horse Publications, 1991. 271 pages.

Drummond, Marcy. *Long Distance Riding.* New York: Howell Book House, 1987. 141 pages.

Morris, Arlene. *Be Trail Ready: A Manual for the Beginning Trail or Distance Rider.* Boise, ID: Morris Endurance Enterprises.

Oltmann, Hesselgesser, Stillman, and Lewis. *Fit to Finish: The Distance Rider's Guide to Personal Fitness and Nutrition.* 1990. 126 pages.

Pacific Coast Equestrian Research Farm. *Endurance and Competitive Trail Riding Manual.* Badger, CA: Pacific Coast Equestrian Research Farm, 1967.

Snow, D. H. and C. J. Vogel. *Equine Fitness: The Care and Training of the Athletic Horse.* North Pomfret, VT: David & Charles Inc, 1987. 271 pages.

Tellington, Wentworth and Linda Tellington-Jones. *Endurance and Competitive Trail Riding.* Garden City, NY: Doubleday & Co., 1979. 314 pages.

Trail Riding Equiment and Suppliers

Easyboots and E-Z Ride Stirrups. EasyCare, Inc.
1600 E. Hanley #136, Tucson, AZ 85737
(520) 297-9600.

Running Bear Tack and Equipment for the LD Rider
1348 Township Road 256, Kitts Hill, OH 45645
www.runningbear.com

Cool Tack Endurance and Tack Equipment
1000 Sevier Road, Cool, CA 95614
www.cooltack.com

Canadian Trail House
Box 5368, Devon Alberta, Canada T9G 1Y1
www.biothanetack

Hought Fine Art & Leather
P.O. Box 2115, McKinleyville, CA 95519
(707) 839-1164 / 1-800-839-1164
www.hought.com/endthg.html

Dixon Smith Equestrian Clothing
P.O. Box 586, Mullumbimby NSW 2482
Australia
www.dixonsmith.com.au

Griffins Tack
Dona and Henry Griffin
9110 Iroquois Trail, Stagecoach, NV 89429
www.griffinstack.com/other.htm

Desoto Custom Saddlery
1720 West 36 Mile Road, Boon, MI 49618
www.desotosaddle.com

Advanced Equine Products
5004-228th Avenue S.E.
Issaquah, WA 98029
www.advancedequine.com/endurance/

Buford Saddle and Tack Co.
Rt. 1 Box 226, Big Cabin, OK 74332
(918) 783-5715
www.bufordsaddle.com/saddles/west/west.htm

Two Horse Enterprises
P.O. Box 15517, Fremont, CA 94539
www.twohorseenterprises.com

Long Riders Gear
575 Price Street, Ste. 106, Pismo Beach, CA 93449
www.longridersgear.com

Trail-Rite Ranch and Products
Tammy and Charlie Robinson
18171 Lost Creek Road, Saugus, CA 91350
(661) 513-9269
www.trail-rite.com

Fabtron Trail Saddles and Tack Supply
3806 E. Lamar Alexander Pkwy.
Maryville, TN 37804
www.fabtron.com

Have Saddle Will Travel
1-800-821-3607
www.havesaddlewilltravel.com

Higher Mark (free catalog of biothane trail equipment)
12825 NE 9th St., Silver Springs, FL 34488
www.highermark.com

KV Vet Supply
1-800-423-8211
www.kvvet.com

Outback Trading Company (oilskin parkas)
(610) 931-5141
www.outbacktrading.com

Stagecoach West
Routes 5 and 20, Irving, New York 14081
1-800-648-1121
www.stagecoachwest.com

Trail and Pleasure Riding Supplies
212 Myrtle Ct., Taylorsville, KY 40071
www.trailandpleasure.com

Trail's End
1-800-758-6344
www.4trailsend.com

The Australian Connection
1-800-847-8521
www.theaustralianconnection.com

Organizations

The American Trail Horse Association
P.O. Box 293, Courtland, IL 60112
wwww.TrailHorse.com

American Trails Organization
Publishes *Trails Tracks* Newsletter
www.AmericanTrails.org

Back Country Horseman of America
Box 1192, Columbia Falls, MT 59912

Equestrian Land Conservation Resource is dedicated to promoting access to land for equestrian use. www.elcr.org,

American Trails is a national trails advocacy organization whose website lists trails state by state. www.outdoorlink.com/amtrails/

Ride and Tie Association
11734 Wolf Rd, Grass Valley, CA 95949
(916) 268-8474

Western States Trail Foundation
701 High St., #228C, Auburn, CA 95603
(916) 823-7282

Breed Associations
Some breed associations organize group rides.

The American Quarter Horse Association sponsors over 70 rides a year and they welcome all horses. www.aqha.com/recreation/ride/index.html

The American Paint Horse Association also sponsors trail rides that are open to all horses. www.apha.com/trailrides/index.html

The National Park Service
Extremely helpful to riders who want to explore NP trails. Go to their website and follow the link to the specific park you want to visit. You will find plenty of valuable information. If you need additional help, send the park an e-mail and ask for horse information, maps and any specific thing that you need to know. They will tell you where you can ride and the places you are allowed to camp with horses.
www.nps.gov

Websites on Trails and Trail Riding

Two Horse Enterprises
www.extendinc.com/twohorse/index.htm
Miscellaneous equipment, books and maps of trails in many states.

Equisearch
www.equisearch.com/sports/trailriding
This carries a number of trail riding articles as well as other disciplines.

The Long Rider's Guild
www.thelongridersguild.com
A very entertaining website with many stories of people who have ridden 1,000 miles or more on a single trip. It includes stories from people who are traveling right now from all over the world.

www.fastehorses.com/aerctrails.
Candid forum for trail issues.

Trail Training for Horse and Rider
www.trailtraining.bigstep.com.
The author's e-newsletter. Here you can sign up for my free e-newsletter and read past newsletters on-line.

www.hikercentral.com/riding/.
A guide to public parks and lands.

Info on trail riding and travel. www.horsetravels.com.

Contains helpful information on trail riding, trail manners, and training. www.roundpenmagic.com.

Camping and Trail Information

For information on different trails throughout the country and places to camp with your horse, I found two very useful websites:

Horse & Mule Trail Guide USA
www.horseandmuletrails.com

Horse Trails and Campgrounds Directory
www.horsetraildirectory.com

Beyond Just Trail Riding

Mounted Orienteering

Ten paper plates called Objective Stations are placed in an area of two to twelve square miles. Riders are given a map, and with the help of a compass and landmark clues, they locate each Objective Station and write down the secret code numbers as proof that they have been there. Most rides have a maximum time of six hours. Horses must be in good shape and be capable trail horses.
For information, contact:
National Association of Competitive Mounted Orienteering
Walter H. Olsen
503 171st Ave SE
Tenino, WA 98589-9711
Website: www.nacmo.com

Mounted Search and Rescue

Most states have groups of volunteers who train their horses and themselves for mounted search and rescue. They will assist in looking for missing people, articles and evidence. Some groups also participate in parades, drill teams and trail rides. Check your local communities to see what is available in your area. A website that lists groups by state is www.ibiblio.org/msar.

Group and Charity Rides

Many communities have organizations that host rides to raise money for charity. Check your local tack shop's bulletin board and regional publications to see what is happening in your area.

Endurance Riding and Competitive Trail Riding

If you want to compete your horse, you may want to try Endurance or Competitive Trail Riding. Endurance rides are judged by the fastest sound horse to finish. Competitive Trail Rides are judged on the fittest horse to complete a distance within a specified amount of time.

An ideal place for information on Endurance Riding is:
The American Endurance Ride Conference
P.O. Box 6027
Auburn, CA 95604
www.aerc.org

They also have a wonderful website for beginners to endurance riding
www.Endurance.net/newbie

Information on Competitive Trail Riding can be found at:
North American Trail Ride Conference
P.O. Box 224
Sedalia, CO 80135
www.natrc.org